The Promise
of
Tillich

The Promise of Theology
Martin E. Marty, General Editor

BX 4827. T53
T25 1971

The Promise
of
Tillich

by

L. GORDON TAIT

ST. FRANCIS SEMINARY
SALZMANN
LIBRARY
Milwaukee, Wis. 53207

WITHDRAWN

J. B. LIPPINCOTT COMPANY
Philadelphia and New York

Copyright © 1971 by L. Gordon Tait

All rights reserved

First edition

Printed in the United States of America

Library of Congress Catalog Card No.: 79-146687

The University of Chicago Press has kindly permitted the quotation of
many passages from Paul Tillich's *Systematic Theology*, which is copy-
righted as follows: Volume I copyright 1951 by The University of
Chicago, all rights reserved. Volume II © 1957 by The University of
Chicago, all rights reserved. Volume III © 1963 by The University of
Chicago, all rights reserved.

To Lois

Foreword

While this study appears at the close of a series on the promise of various thinkers, its subject, Paul Tillich, actually inspired the whole conception. Near the end of his life a group of young thinkers began to dismiss his work. As an old controversialist, Tillich had no difficulty understanding opposition to his system; he thrived on give-and-take. As a religious socialist and an anti-Nazi in Germany, he had been involved in life-and-death struggles. He did not shun antagonists. But he could not comprehend the young people who professed to see nothing worth discussing at all.

The media were showing interest in the attacks on the man who, perhaps more than any other, had helped form the thought of a whole generation of American religious thinkers, even though he came to these shores at mid-career and dealt in what were at first unfamiliar categories. Through the years he had succeeded in making these categories our own. But now, whether in mere Oedipal reaction, or to clear space for themselves and their work, or in honest disagreement, they wanted not only to move beyond him but also not to discuss him at all.

He was not alone: Karl Barth, Rudolf Bultmann, Reinhold Niebuhr, and others of the generation of theological giants were also being set aside. In the process an even younger generation was being guided *past* their thought.

Tillich was vulnerable to the charges of his attackers. His system was grounded in an idealism which was unattractive in philosophical circles in our time. The Anglo-American world, devoted as its philosophers were to language analysis and the empirical schools, was not at home with his "Being"-philosophy. Perhaps he had been building on a condemned site.

Still, the edifice itself was so impressive and the man was so passionate and so profound that it seemed hard to begin to speak of moving past him so soon. The "promise of theology" books set out to explore what in the work of men like this was still in advance of us.

By now it seems clear that, however much correction and revision of Tillich must go on, his influence remains strong and many of his concepts and insights will remain, no matter how his system as a whole is regarded. Certainly no one of his existential depth or creative power has risen to take his place.

In the pages that follow, Professor Tait gives an account of Tillich's life and main themes and then offers suggestions concerning which of these ought to be pursued by people tomorrow. I commend you to his guidance.

MARTIN E. MARTY
The University of Chicago

Contents

I.
Life in the Boundary Situation

When Paul Tillich died in 1965 at the age of seventy-nine, he was one of America's greatest theologians. Author of innumerable books and articles, teacher of thousands of students, speaker and preacher standing behind countless lecterns and pulpits across the land, he expressed fresh and penetrating ideas, directed to life, far-reaching in their implications. They were not standard-brand ideas—pedestrian, superficial, mild; they were quality ideas—creative, profound, demanding.

Paul Tillich was a most compelling man, not just because of his ideas but because of his person. His theology has sometimes been called existential, and that it was. But the striking thing is the way his ideas were one with his life. He could speak to and for modern man because modern man's pains and joys were his. He was a kind of twentieth-century Everyman with his theology pivoting around his own life and being. His words held meaning for ever so many moderns because their experiences were his. Small wonder he captivated so many!

Tillich himself has told us how to approach him. Throughout his life he saw himself as a man living his existence "on the boundary."[1] The boundary concept is a rich one for Tillich, covering his intellectual and personal development. It is the condition within which one moves from one position to another and then back again, a "back-and-forth" experience which results in a new position where one can remain for a time without being tied down tightly. It is the basis of creativity; it presupposes always being receptive to new possibilities. Life in the boundary situation is difficult, dangerous, tense, exciting—but fruitful and rewarding.

One particular boundary situation lay "between native and alien land," between Germany and America. America might like to claim Tillich for her own, but it is important to remember that America was but one side of a crucial boundary situation. For forty-seven years Germany, not America, was home for this pivotal figure in theology. America can take partial credit for helping Paul Tillich attain the pre-eminent position in the world that was his, but not all. The German years were formative and decisive.

GERMANY

Paul Johannes Tillich was born on August 21, 1886, in Starzeddel, Germany, a small industrial town in the province of Brandenburg. If one considers that the nineteenth century did not end until 1914, then Tillich can lay claim, as he did, to bridging two centuries. He grew up surrounded by relatively peaceful and stable conditions, the liberalism and the unbroken cultural traditions of the nineteenth century. This environment was all the more vivid in the case of the young Tillich, since he lived in three small towns with long histories before moving to Berlin with his family in 1900.

When Paul was four years of age, his father, Johannes, a Lutheran pastor, was made superintendent of the district, a kind of head minister over a group of parishes. This meant moving to the town of Schönfliess in eastern Brandenburg. From Paul's twelfth to his fourteenth year he lived in still another town, Königsberg-Neumark, while he attended the *Gymnasium* (high school plus the first two years of college).

Looking back on those early years, Tillich made some interesting observations. He says that quite early a romantic trend began to take shape, an aesthetic attitude to nature. There was a strong, almost mystical attachment to the earth, field, forest, weather, and, in particular, the sea. Year after year Tillich spent his vacations beside the Baltic Sea with its unending horizon and its steady beat of waves upon the shore, and it was clearly by design that when he came to America he purchased a house for vacations and retirement in East Hampton, Long Island, within view of the Atlantic Ocean. It is a fact that much of Tillich's writing was done among trees or by the sea.

Tillich's romanticism was linked to a prevailing sense of history, stemming from his life as a boy in towns still medieval in character. History was a living reality, not dull facts divorced from present experience. The Middle Ages had special value in his emerging romanticism.

[12]

The beautiful Gothic church in Schönfliess, in which his father was a successful pastor for fourteen years, contained more than mere romantic, historical appeal. Tillich's religious upbringing in this church, in a pastor's home, and in a Lutheran elementary school gave him a sense of the holy which was determinative for his later method in theology and philosophy, by which he began with man's experience of the holy and then moved to the divine, not the other way around. The religious influences of those early years forever impressed on him the primary quality of a person's experience of the divine, which made it very easy for him later to appreciate Friedrich Schleiermacher, the nineteenth-century German Protestant theologian who held that religion was based on feeling and intuition, and defined it as "a sense and taste for the infinite."

But the pastor's son grew up experiencing narrowness and limitations, too. The towns seemed cut off from the larger world and transportation was primitive, but even worse were the psychological and sociological restrictions: Prussian authoritarianism in society, Lutheran paternalism in the home, heavy-handed discipline in the schools, and, for good measure, the army, whose influence was pervasive. It was not until after the First World War, Tillich has explained, that he was able to overcome this authoritarian style of life and begin to live as a free, responsible person.

Both parents were strong, but contrasting, personalities. They came from different parts of Germany and exemplified varied approaches to life, in their own way creating another boundary situation for their child as he tried to live between two temperaments. His father represented the East German type, one who is conscientious, dignified, and conservative, with a marked preference for authority and tradition; his mother, the West German type, one who is more liberal, sentimental, and democratic, with a zest for life and love of the concrete. Paul Tillich's mother died early in his life, so his father's influence was the greater. This had the effect of causing many struggles with his father, some of these being extreme in nature. The character of his mother's world was not to be put down that easily.

In 1900 Pastor Tillich was called to an important post in Berlin, and when the family took up residence in the capital young Paul was again sent to a humanistic *Gymnasium,* where the main subjects were Greek and Latin. Upon his graduation in 1904, he attended the Universities of Berlin, Tübingen and Halle to study theology. In time he passed his theological examinations and in 1912 was ordained as a pastor of the Evangelical Lutheran Church.

Even before taking up his theological studies, he had studied philosophy on his own, acquiring a good knowledge of the history of philosophy and a basic knowledge of Kant and Fichte. Schleiermacher, Hegel, and Schelling were the philosophers he studied at the university, with Schelling getting most of the attention. Schelling was of immense importance in the development of Tillich's theological and philosophical ideas, because it was in him that Tillich saw occurring the changeover from Hegelian idealism to the modern existentialist movement.

Tillich was then drawn to Søren Kierkegaard, the nineteenth-century Danish philosopher who opposed the Hegelian dialectic with his own interpretation of man "existing before God." Tillich found Kierkegaard's dialectical psychology and his concept of man impressive in their application. In the years before World War I the full impact of Kierkegaard's interpretation was not widely felt, but in the 1920s he became the saint of both German philosophers and theologians.

The other philosopher who came to have an influence on Tillich was Martin Heidegger.[2] Tillich and Heidegger were at the University of Marburg in the 1920s, Tillich beginning in 1925 to work on his *Systematic Theology* (Volume I was not completed until 1951), and Heidegger writing that classic existentialist statement, *Sein und Zeit (Being and Time)*. There is no indication of how close Tillich and Heidegger were at Marburg, but there is very little doubt that Heidegger's insights were key ones for Tillich. Heidegger, in spite of his emphatic atheism, had a view of man which was very similar to the Christian interpretation of human existence, Tillich claimed. Yet he did not make Heidegger's thought his own, and it is not the easiest thing to judge the extent to which Tillich is a true existentialist. Relative to the discovery of existentialism at Marburg, Tillich has written: "It took years before I became fully aware of the impact of this encounter on my own thinking. I resisted, I tried to learn. I accepted the new way of thinking more than the answers it gave."[3]

Martin Kähler, one of Tillich's professors at Halle, was the theologian who made the greatest impression on him. Kähler's impact was twofold. First, he understood the problem of doubt, putting it within the context of justification by grace through faith; that is, the acceptance and forgiveness of a person in spite of his sin. For Kähler the message of justification applied to the inner moral acts of man, and to his inner intellectual acts as well. Not only the sinner, but the *doubter* (doubt is simply the intellectual form of sin), is accepted by God! Tillich confessed that it was Martin Kähler more than any other person who taught him that doubt does not necessarily separate us from God. The Halle professor helped in another way—in his approach to the problem of historical criticism of the Bible. More directly, what is the relationship between the historical Jesus and the Christ of faith? Kähler himself did not believe that the two must be separated. His statement, though not definitive, is beneficial because in the nineteenth century he pointed a prophetic finger toward the problems of radical criticism in the twentieth century.

The year 1914 found Pastor Paul Tillich in Berlin. There was a hasty marriage which later ended in divorce. At the outbreak of war in August, 1914, the young pastor enlisted in the German army as a chaplain. He served from September, 1914, to September, 1918, but it took him only a few months to arrive at the sobering conclusion that the war would last indefinitely and would be the ruin of all Europe. He also quickly observed that the apparent unity of Germany was a myth and that, in reality, the nation was split into conflicting classes, the workers regarding the church as consistently favoring the ruling class. A short-lived revolution did occur in which imperial Germany collapsed. The war marked a turning point in Tillich's thinking. He saw that there would be no easy return to normal patterns of thought. In fact, he could even specify a certain long, horrible night in 1915, during the Battle of Champagne, when, as he put it, "I walked along the rows of dying men, and much of my German classical philosophy broke down that night. . . ."[4]

After the war he found himself in company with other intellectuals organizing a movement known as "Religious Socialism." They sensed that they were entering upon a new period of history, a time of *kairos*—the Greek word in the New Testament for "fullness of time," a moment in which the eternal breaks into the temporal order and the temporal is prepared to receive it. Religious Socialism was not a political party, though it called for a certain amount of political action; nor was it a religious organization, though it was based to a certain extent on Christian principles. It tried to give socialism a religious depth, for the basic assumption was that no planned society could avoid its eventual destruction unless it had a religious foundation.

Religious Socialism faded. The *kairos* did not materialize. Instead, Nazism, Fascism and Communism arose. Despite these discouraging developments, Tillich never lost confidence. As late as 1952 he declared that if the prophetic message is valid at all, "there is nothing beyond religious socialism."

The post-World War I years also saw Tillich becoming interested in Karl Marx. He regarded Marx, mainly, as one of the leading modern teachers of the truth about human existence.[5] Marx compares with Freud in that both men turned their faces away from the superficial, balanced idealism of the nineteenth century. Tillich also discovered in Marxism a deep, prophetic passion, a genuine expectation that society would be drastically transformed and significantly reconstructed. Karl Marx's preoccupation with economic materialism and the transformation of society was proof enough for Tillich that Marx was actually dealing in theological profundities: man lives on earth (in existence), not in heaven (in essence).

But there was approval with reservation. If there is a *Yes,* there is always a *No.* Tillich gave his assessment of Marx in dialectical fashion, declaring, "The Yes was based on the prophetic, humanistic and realistic elements in Marx's passionate style and profound thought, the No on the calculating, materialistic, and resentful elements in Marx's analysis, polemics, and propaganda."[6]

Paul Tillich began his academic career in 1919 as a *Privatdozent,* or free-lance lecturer, at the University of Berlin, introducing class discussion when it was unheard of there, and covering a whole supermarket of subjects in his lectures from 1919 to 1924—the relation of religion to politics, art, philosophy, depth psychology and sociology. It was a concentrated effort to create a theology which would engage in constructive conversation with various cultural components. He was, very consciously, beginning to develop his own role, that of standing on the "boundary line," and his own theology, a "theology of culture."

The particular social milieu was conducive to Tillich's enterprise. In Berlin in the postwar years political problems seemed to be matters of life and death; social structures appeared to be dissolving; authority, education, family, sex, friendship, and pleasure all seemed to be in a state of creative chaos. In addition to Religious Socialism, two new movements—art and psychoanalysis—drew Tillich to them. The depth psychology of Freud and his followers was discovered to be extremely worthwhile for a theological understanding of man. The insights gained from depth psychology highlighted man's existential predicament, raising the vital question of his very existence, the question to which Tillich felt theology must be forever addressing itself.

Tillich was introduced to modern art and Hannah Werner about the same time. Berlin in the 1920s was a lighthearted, bright, lively city, and *Privatdozent* Tillich was not one to stay home at night. One evening there was a fancy-dress ball sponsored by the art students, which he attended in cutaway and turban. There he met a handsome girl, Hannah Werner, whose costume featured long green silk stockings. To use his own words, "Things went on from there," eventually to marriage in March, 1924. Paul and Hannah had two children, René Descartes and Erdmuthe Christiane, both of whom are living in the United States.

Tillich's appreciation of art had its beginning during his military service, when he found release from the horrors of war by spending his leisure time studying art. His appreciation only increased in the years after the war. With his wife, an art student, he made a three-month walking trip through parts of Italy, discovering the riches of Italian medieval and Renaissance art and architecture. Tillich was just as deeply moved by the German expressionism of the early twentieth century, seeing in the works of the expressionists power, ecstasy, mystical fullness and metaphysical significance.

Therefore, it was not just enjoyment or some kind of aesthetic experience which gave art its significance. Art, Tillich believed, holds within itself another of those boundary situations, the boundary between religion and culture. Art reveals, much better than science and philosophy can, the inmost character of a spiritual situation. The symbols of art have "something of a revelatory character while scientific conceptualization must suppress the symbolic in favor of objective adequacy."[7] The mosaics of Ravenna, the ceiling paintings of the Sistine Chapel, the portraits of the older Rembrandt—all these can put the viewer right in the middle of the religion and culture boundary situation; because if one has been deeply moved, as Tillich was by these artistic expressions, he is hard put to say whether his experience was cultural or religious. It might well be both; that is:

It might be correct to say that the experience is cultural in form and religious in substance [content]. It is cultural because it is not attached to a specific ritual act; but it is religious because it touches on the question of the Absolute and the limits of human existence.... Culture is religious wherever human existence is subjected to ultimate questions and thus transcended; and wherever unconditioned meaning becomes visible in works that have only conditioned meaning in themselves. In experiencing the substantially religious character of culture I came to the boundary between religion and culture, and I have never left it.[8]

After almost five years at Berlin, Dr. Tillich became, officially, Professor Tillich when he moved to a theological professorship at the University of Marburg, and then in rather quick succession to university philosophy or theology positions ("As a theologian I tried to remain a philosopher, and conversely so") in Dresden, Leipzig, and Frankfurt (1929-33). It has already been noted that at Marburg Tillich was introduced to the Heidegger brand of existentialism. A new brand of theology, Neo-orthodoxy, was now in vogue; it was associated with the name of Karl Barth, a leading twentieth-century Swiss Protestant theologian. When such neo-orthodox motifs as the sovereignty of God, the centrality of revelation in Christ, the authority of the Bible, man as sinner, began to have their effect on the theological students, Tillich complained that cultural problems came to be excluded from the theological purview, German theologians such as Schleiermacher, Harnack, Troeltsch, and Otto[9] were contemptuously rejected, and all social and political ideas were eliminated from theological discussions.

Even though both Barth and Tillich had been greatly influenced by Kierkegaard, they disagreed on some basic points. Tillich did approve of Barth for producing a theology that stressed the unchanging truth of revelation over against the changing demands of the situation, but Tillich could not tolerate the sharp separation between theology and culture upon which Barth and other Neo-orthodox theologians were insisting. For Tillich's part, the trouble was that Barth's theology hurled the timeless message at the human situation like a stone, and because it sought no common ground with those in the human situation, it ran the danger of being irrelevant. Tillich's position was that the person first listens attentively to the questions of human existence buried in the temporal situation and *then* responds with the power of the timeless message. This is what Tillich calls "apologetic" or "answering theology," a theology which seeks to find the common ground between the message and the situation by listening first to the questions posed before answering in terms of the message. There is a concomitant danger in this plan; namely, that the message gets distorted when fitted to prior questions. Be that as it may, Paul Tillich unhesitatingly chose an apologetic or answering theology for two reasons, one a fact and the other a personal conviction. The fact: that for the last two centuries the central problem of theology has been the adaptation of the Christian faith to the modern mind. The conviction: that a synthesis between message and situation is possible and necessary if Christianity is to avoid becoming a museum piece and if civilization is not to disintegrate.[10]

AMERICA

If one side of the boundary situation "between native and alien land" was Germany, the other was America. When he arrived in New York on November 4, 1933, Tillich was virtually unknown except to a select group of philosophers and theologians. Tillich's promising career in Germany had come to an abrupt end. On a certain day in the winter of 1931-32 a gang of over three hundred of Hitler's Brown Shirts raided the University of Frankfurt where he was teaching philosophy and beat up some radical students. In the investigation which followed the incident, Tillich registered his strong objections to the actions of the Nazi thugs. Later he reported, "I had the honor to be the first non-Jewish professor dismissed from a German University."[11]

Reinhold Niebuhr, professor of theology and ethics at Union Theological Seminary in New York City, happened to be in Germany during the summer of 1933 and invited Tillich to come to America and teach theology at the seminary. After some hesitation, he accepted.

To begin a new life in a strange land at the age of forty-seven without any knowledge of English was no easy undertaking for the new immigrant, and he admitted years later that without the help of students and faculty at Union Seminary, and the assistance of German and American friends, his entrance into American life might have been a disaster. In time, Tillich mastered English and became an American citizen (1940), returning to Europe only for brief visits.[12]

Paul Tillich took this new and difficult boundary situation and over the years created a distinguished theological career at Union Theological Seminary (1933-55), Harvard University (1955-62) and the University of Chicago (1962-65). He was forever grateful to Union for taking him in "as a stranger" and providing a community of life and work and worship for his first twenty-two years in the United States. In many respects Union Seminary in New York City was an ideal location for Tillich. In contrast to the individualism of academic life in Germany, Tillich found a community of professors, students, and staff, often with their families. It was a close-knit but not a closed-off community. There was, and is, a continuous flow of visitors from all kinds of backgrounds passing through Union's quadrangle, resulting in a worldwide theological, cultural and political outlook. Tillich found what others have found, that it was nearly impossible to remain provincial in such a cosmopolitan setting.[13]

But New York City was just as stimulating as Union. Tillich always loved the city. It was not that he rejected the country; in fact, another of his boundary situations was "between city and country," and this was just as true of life in America as it was in Germany. As a boy living in a small town, he savored the rare trip to Berlin with the dynamic character of its life—the heavy traffic, the crowds of people, the changing scenes. And it was no different when he came to live in New York City years later, or when he moved to Cambridge or Chicago; the same aesthetic appreciation of the city was present. The city, Tillich once explained, is important for the development of the critical side of intellectual and artistic life and provides firsthand knowledge of political and social movements.[14] Thus he commented, "I always considered it a good destiny that the emigration of the year 1933 brought me to New York, the largest of all large cities."[15]

In America Tillich maintained, at least until 1945, his political interests that had occupied a large part of his life in Germany.[16] There were the active relationship with the Graduate Faculty of Political Science at New York's New School for Social Research, his chairmanship of the Council for a Democratic Germany during World War II, his chairmanship of the organization known as Self-Help for Emigrés from Central Europe, and his general interest and participation in the religious-socialist cause in the United States. He never did lose interest in politics, and his efforts on behalf of world peace are not to be overlooked; but his active participation in American political affairs, and especially after the Second World War, did not compare with the earlier involvement in German affairs before 1933. Meanwhile, he turned to other aspects of culture in America and to the work of expounding his theology.

Although the key themes and the general outline of Tillich's mature thought had already been intimated before he left Germany, it was in America that he developed his impressive theological system—in two forms: his three-volume *Systematic Theology* and his more popular writings, books such as *The Protestant Era, Dynamics of Faith,* and *The Courage to Be,* articles, essays, sermons, and addresses. The same basic themes and terms—the ground of being, ultimate concern, theonomy, kairos, dimension of depth, estrangement, the courage to be, the New Being in Christ—appear in both his popular and technical works.

Some new problems faced a German emigré wanting to write serious theology in the United States.[17] Tillich found it rather disconcerting to read a theoretical paper, even to an educated group, and at the end he asked: "What shall we do about it?" He was discovering firsthand what he calls "the pragmatic-experiential approach of American theology," which is derived from emphasizing the realization of the Kingdom of God in history over against the stress on pure doctrine in German Lutheranism. In Europe the church's main interest was the problem of its ultimate foundation, theology was supposed to explain this foundation systematically, and preaching and sacraments were vital. In America the church was a social agent; foundations were taken for granted, so the practical demands were placed first. The church existed to make better people and better social conditions. Coinciding with this understanding of the church was the American "nominalist attitude," a concern for the particular rather than for absolute principle. This may engender an admirable tentativeness and humility toward ultimate truth, but it can and often does, Tillich warned, result in a rejection of any search for such ultimacy. America also tended not to be serious about history. Tillich put it this way: "It was one of our most important tasks to balance the American emphasis on new beginning with the European emphasis on tradition. And it was equally important to balance the American emphasis on facts with the European emphasis on interpretation."[18]

For approximately twenty years Paul Tillich worked away with a minimum of public acclaim. Then rather quickly in the 1950s wider recognition was accorded him, and he became known as one of America's foremost theologians. His days thereafter were full ones, occupied by teaching, lecturing, preaching, discussing, and writing. As his fame spread, there were times when he seemed to be everywhere at once, on the go continually.

One of Tillich's theological colleagues from another city knocked at the door of his New York apartment one evening. Upon entering, he found the living room occupied by people he did not recognize, but who were having an exciting conversation with one another and with Tillich. It was obvious that the people present were psychiatrists and psychologists. A woman remarked to the new arrival, "If you are surprised to see me here, you are not half so surprised as I am to find myself here. If a month ago someone had said to me, 'You are going to spend an evening at the home of a theologian,' I would have dismissed him with dispatch and perhaps even with contempt, but here I am tonight."[19]

Tillich once wrote, "I do not think that it is possible today to elaborate a Christian doctrine of man ... without using the immense material brought forth by depth psychology."[20] The relationship between the theological and (depth) psychological views of man absorbed much of Tillich's time and intellectual energy. Nowhere is this more evident than in the William Ellery Channing Lecture he delivered in Chicago in May, 1954, entitled "Psychoanalysis, Existentialism and Theology."[21] He began this lecture by noting that the common root of existentialism and psychoanalysis is the protest against the philosophy of consciousness which became paramount in modern industrial society, achieving a veritable victory in Descartes. Protests against this type of philosophy were centered in Pascal, Hamann, Schopenhauer, Nietzsche, Kierkegaard, Marx and others, but it was Freud who, in his discovery of the unconscious, helped significantly to combat the philosophy of consciousness.

Basically, depth psychology and existentialism are concerned with man's existential predicament in contrast to his essential nature. The focus in both depth psychology and existentialism is man's estranged existence in all its aspects and implications.

When one moves to theology, Tillich continues, definite existential themes can be located, themes such as the original goodness of everything including man, the fall which constitutes the transition from essential goodness to existential estrangement from oneself, and the possibility of salvation or healing or making whole once again. On the other hand, the growth of existentialism and depth psychology is of inestimable value for theology. For one thing, these movements helped theology rediscover the vast depth psychological material in the religious literature of the last two thousand years. For another, theology rediscovered that sin is separation, estrangement from one's essential being, not the sum total of immoral or disapproved acts. Third, these movements helped theology find again the demonic structures that are so influential in determining our consciousness and our decisions. Fourth, theology had to relearn a lesson from the psychoanalytic method; that is, "the meaning of forgiveness as acceptance of those who are unacceptable and not of those who are the good people." And lastly, theology has to come up with the answer, by means of religious symbols, to the question of human existence. Tillich's conclusion? "Existentialists and analysts themselves do not need to know that they have given to theology these [tremendous gifts]. But the theologians should know it."[22]

At Harvard University one day, Tillich, wearing his French beret, moved slowly down the long steps from Widener Library and made his way across the Yard to Emerson D, where students were gathering for his lecture. By the time he started to lecture, the number of students was so great that they were sitting in the aisles and on the platform. The students concentrated on every word the professor uttered; the professor, then in his seventies, transmitted an obvious empathy for his youthful listeners.

As he meditated on his role as teacher at Harvard, he claimed that he saw in the lives of many university and college students, not just those at Harvard, feelings of emptiness, insecurity, meaninglessness, guilt; that is, those characteristics of the human predicament portrayed in existentialist literature and art. With a kind of missionary fervor he engaged the forces which gave rise to these feelings, and the response he received assured him that it was in dealing with these facets of the student experience that the larger question of life's meaning—the religious problem—could be considered. Tillich admitted that teaching at Harvard actually strengthened his position on the boundary line of religion and culture, for one of the courses he taught was called just that—"Religion and Culture," offered in the Humanities Department.[23]

In April, 1961, the Massachusetts Institute of Technology held its centennial celebration. Seated on the platform with theologian Tillich, the speaker, were physicist Robert Oppenheimer, Harvard psychologist Jerome Bruner, Dean George Harrison of M.I.T., and novelist Aldous Huxley. Tillich's accusation: that science was corrupting the religion and philosophy of modern man by giving him means without ends. Starting with the Greeks and moving to the present, the speaker surveyed man's *telos*—his "inner aim"—finally declaring that in our time technique has become not merely the means to the end, but the end itself. His question, put sharply to his hearers, was, "Is this not surrender of a *telos* altogether?" His speech ended with the hope that the mounting protest against the dehumanization of man would finally result in a view of man which recognizes the "multi-dimensional unity he is."[24]

In 1963 in New York City, Paul Tillich addressed a large gathering of celebrities on the occasion of *Time* magazine's fortieth anniversary. The subject was "The Ambiguity of Perfection." Speaking to this prestigious group, he explained that the character of the human condition, like that of all life, is "ambiguity," defined as "the inseparable mixture of good and evil, of true and false, of creative and destructive forces—both individual and social." Turning to a more immediate ambiguity, Tillich repeated an earlier observation, that American culture is one-dimensional, ever expanding on the horizontal plane. He warned his hearers that he was not peddling religion, a cultural good, but that he was pleading for the restoration of the vertical dimension, that "state in which we are grasped by the infinite seriousness of the question of the meaning of life." His final exhortation to the audience was to work with passion and wisdom "so that the ultimate question becomes powerful again in our Western culture and in our nation."[2 5]

Tillich was one of the chief speakers at another important meeting in New York in February, 1965. It was a three-day conference on peace attended by nearly two thousand people from fourteen nations. The focus was on Pope John XXIII's encyclical, "Pacem in Terris," and the speakers on the first day included Linus Pauling, Paul-Henri Spaak, Nicolai Inozemstev from *Pravda,* and Paul Tillich.

Tillich spoke of ambiguity again, calling attention to the conflict between the goodness of man's essential being and the ambiguity of his actual being, and he wanted the appeal for peace directed to all men, not just to "all men of good will" as the encyclical stated. Man's moral nature is ambiguous, he declared, so that in the best will there is an element of bad will, and in the worst will there is an element of good will. Thus, a genuine, realistic hope must always be distinguished from utopian expectations. A genuine hope does not point forward to a final period in history in which peace and justice rule. "History is fulfilled in the great moments in which something new is created. . . . [Hence] we can hope for partial victories over the forces of evil in a particular moment of time."[2 6]

In the spring of 1961, Tillich preached in the James Memorial Chapel of Union Theological Seminary. The sermon title was "Spiritual Presence,"[2 7] and the text was II Corinthians 3:5-6. Dressed in a simple black robe, he told his congregation that Divine Spirit means "God present to our spirit"; it is God Himself as present in communities and personalities, grasping, inspiring, transforming them.

For Spirit is first of all power, the power that drives the human spirit above itself towards what it cannot attain by itself, the love that is greater than all other gifts, the truth in which the depth of being opens itself to us, the holy that is the manifestation of the presence of the ultimate. . . .

But there are other conscious and noticeable manifestations of the Spiritual Presence. Let me enumerate some of them, while you ask yourselves whether and to what degree they are of your own experience. The Spirit can work in you with a soft but insistent voice, telling you that your life is empty and meaningless, but that there are chances of a new life waiting before the door of your inner self to fill its void and to conquer its dullness. The Spirit can work in you, awakening the desire to strive towards the sublime against the profanity of the average day. The Spirit can give you the courage that says "yes" to life in spite of the destructiveness you have experienced around you and within you. The Spirit can reveal to you that you have hurt somebody deeply, but it also can give you the right word that reunites him with you. The Spirit can make you love, with the divine love, someone you profoundly dislike or in whom you have no interest. The Spirit can conquer your sloth towards what you know is the aim of your life, and it can transform your moods of aggression and depression into stability and serenity. . . .

These are the works of the Spirit, signs of the Spiritual Presence with us and in us. In view of these manifestations, who can assert that he is without Spirit? Who can say that he is in no way a bearer of the Spirit?[28]

PERSON AND RESPONSE

It is one thing to make speeches and preach sermons; it is something else when people listen—but it is something far greater when people listen and take to heart what has been said. It was not that everyone agreed, because Tillich had critics among his many admirers. But he was a man who could not be brushed aside easily; his words and ideas had a quiet, coat-sleeve-tugging insistence about them. Professor Paul Tillich was the one theologian who for over a quarter of a century could speak to Americans of every description[29] about "the ultimate question" of human existence—"What am I?"—in such a way that they would take seriously what he said.

As a person, this illustrious thinker and teacher possessed an unsurpassing presence and charm. He was tall, rather thin, and until the end of his life stood very erect. He spoke English slowly with only a trace of an accent in later years. His voice was soft. His face was strong. His eyes, behind glasses of clear-plastic rims, were alert. His hair was wavy and white.

And then there was the intellect, the power and brilliance of the man's intellect. His mind was broad, analytic and creative.[30] He drew from several deep wells, that of classical learning, of broad reading, and of keen perception of human beings and human events. The vast knowledge was never used in a hit-or-miss fashion; it was organized, focused knowledge used effectively to expand or illustrate or criticize an idea. One of his colleagues employs the figure of a "fugue unfolding" to describe the way this original thinker designed and executed an article or a lecture.[31] But what set Tillich's mind apart from so many others was his creativity. He did not spend time analyzing certain segments of history or the ideas of other men. He was too absorbed in creating his own system, his own broad vision of reality, to putter about with lesser stuff. His ideas, thus, were creative, profound, demanding. Many of us who heard him, though we might not have immediately understood or even agreed with everything he said, were grasped by the man and amazed at the power and brilliance of his mind.

There were other qualities. His manner was unassuming, not shy; authoritative, not aggressive. A man of considerable patience, he generally encountered people forthrightly in the effort to communicate successfully. He responded best to those persons who took him seriously, especially inquiring students, and his concern for intellectual integrity enabled him to pick out a "phony" a long way off. He reserved his particular disdain for those who were only on the prowl for a new leader to worship. His sense of honesty extended to the kinds of questions directed to him. Constantly playing with a large paper clip ("my fetish," he called it), he would try to answer any question put to him—there was no question too sacrosanct or too banal—as long as it was asked honestly. In any discussion Tillich preferred sharp differences and even unresolved tension over the avoidance of disagreement or the striving for a genial consensus.

Tillich was no joyless, academic recluse. He was vigorous, operating with a kind of unquenchable zeal, totally committed to spreading his message to one and all. There was the side of him which produced the abstract thought, but the other side of the man showed up in the give-and-take of discussion and in friendship with a host of individuals of widely variant types and vocations. For example, one has only to scan the seven-page glossary of names in Tillich's *My Travel Diary: 1936* or check the correspondence in the Tillich

Archives at Harvard Divinity School to see the number and kinds of friends he had. Seldom humorous in his public speeches, in small groups or among friends he could be quite jovial. To his close friends he was known as "Paulus." He loved a glass of good wine and enjoyed dancing. A nicely turned ankle could catch his eye. Chess was a favorite game. He and his wife often dined out with friends or had them in for dinner. Nothing was more enjoyable than socializing with friends. Second only to that was his delight in lively, serious-minded students. He relished an animated bull session and would do his best to get to all the student discussions to which he was invited.

Certainly an outstanding feature of Professor Tillich's career was his charismatic impact on students, theological and nontheological alike. It is easy to ask why; it is harder to answer. On the negative side, he delivered his lectures slowly and steadily, reading them almost word for word. He would take questions and answer them authoritatively. If the way a question was put did not suit him, he would reword it so that it would make sense in his own categories, then he would answer it—in his own categories. Sometimes his speaking schedule around the country was so demanding that he would return exhausted to the campus just in time for a seminar, dozing off during the reading of a boring paper, but arousing himself in time to present his own views on the subject. On the positive side, put simply, there was the man and his mind. His vigor, unassuming manner, honesty, forthrightness, patience, love of students, along with his broad, analytical and creative mind, made all the difference. Somehow, in a way that is hard to explain, he lived in and through his students. He tested out ideas on them, offering them the fruits of his thought and the benefits of his experiences. In a rather surprising way, Paul Tillich conveyed to his students the feeling that he needed them, not to build up his ego but to participate in a learning experience that could be complete only when teacher and student genuinely help each other. A former student and later colleague of Tillich observed, "Teaching was for him a process of love, and so he received love in return."[32]

A final factor in Tillich's acceptance which lies quite outside the man and his mind is to be found in the American situation after World War II. Jerald C. Brauer, a friend of Tillich's and professor at the Divinity School of the University of Chicago, has proposed that right up to the Second World War the United States lived a rich existence, one that was relatively untouched by the world's troubles and still open to a boundless future. After the war, the nation found herself for the first time in a boundary situation which she did not like, hardly knowing what to do. It was a boundary between a recent victory and the immediate appearance of a new enemy; between a technology that would introduce a new age of peace and prosperity and the constant threat of atomic annihilation; between newly acquired power and the frustration of trying to use it creatively; between power and prestige and deep insecurity and meaninglessness. In brief, Paul Tillich, claims Brauer, probably more than any other single figure in America, prepared the American people to live in a boundary situation. He did this, of course, from the religious perspective, but it was a perspective that extended beyond theology to the social, the political, the cultural, and the personal. Finding themselves in a boundary situation for the first time, many Americans turned to one whose life and theology were worked out on the boundary.[33]

However, most Americans did not turn to Tillich in the post-World War II years. Some preferred the gospel of Fulton Sheen or Norman Vincent Peale, or the revivalistic appeal of Billy Graham. Other Americans liked the sound of Paul Tillich, but their understanding and appropriation of such terms as "ultimate concern" and "the courage to be" remained on the level of cocktail party superficiality.

Tillich the theologian is his own man; he defies categorization. When he arrived in the United States, many wanted to associate him with Neo-orthodoxy. Later, there were attempts to make a religious Liberal out of him. Both efforts were unsuccessful, albeit one could observe some affinities between Tillich and each theological school.

The theological reactions to Tillich do not divide cleanly into schools either—for instance, the Tillichians and the anti-Tillichians—although two general responses are evident. There are some thinkers who take sharp issue with one or more of Tillich's main ideas. Karl Barth, the only other modern theologian who has written a broad systematic theology, decisively rejects Tillich's method of first asking the existential question and then giving the religious answer. Christ is no answer to any previous question, asserts Barth. God speaks and acts; He does not await the anticipations of the human mind. American theologian Nels F. S. Ferré, who has always had high respect for Tillich, maintains that Tillich's position cannot be held within the Christian faith without fundamentally altering and destroying it. Says Ferré flatly, "In intellectual honesty a person is Christian or Tillichian, but he cannot be both."[34] Father George H. Tavard, a Roman Catholic theologian who upholds the Christological teaching of the Council of Chalcedon as the norm for both Catholic and Protestant Christians, calls Tillich's Christology deficient because "it is not so much focused on a historical event (the actual coming of Christ in human form) as on a philosophico-religious principle."[35]

Another kind of response is to be seen in the evaluations of Wilhelm Pauck, John Macquarrie and Jerald Brauer. Pauck, a church historian who taught for many years at Union Theological Seminary, regards the three volumes of Tillich's *Systematic Theology* as a constructive work of greatest importance. It "is utterly different from similar works because it bears the marks of having been written by one who . . . had never ceased to think of plans of action for himself and his fellowmen through which a true humanity would be realized. . . ."[36] Contemporary British theologian Macquarrie sees in Tillich (also in Bultmann) the possibility of working out a philosophical basis for religion that makes sense, is contemporary, comprehensive, and capable of further development. "It is a philosophical basis," Macquarrie maintains, "which readily allies itself with the traditional Christian teachings that have inspired Western civilization from its beginnings, revivifying these teachings and making intelligible for our time their abiding truth."[37] Brauer asserts that Tillich's theology meets the most rigorous tests of contemporary relevance and possible survival. In his theology he sketched out the basic issues that are, and will be for a long time, the fundamental questions in Christian theology. "He ventured answers which will continue to be a key station or point of departure on the endless road toward truth. . . . Above all, Paul Tillich made it possible for countless modern men to become or remain Christian without ceasing to be modern men."[38] Vigorous support for such an assessment is found in the words psychoanalyst Rollo May used in his address at the final interment of Tillich's ashes in New Harmony, Indiana, in May, 1966: "The first answer to [the] question of his amazingly wide influence is: *Tillich spoke out of our broken culture, but he spoke believing.* Others spoke out of our broken culture, but with defiance, not affirmation. Others spoke with belief, but from an ethereal philosophic or religious height outside our human culture, which leaves us cold, for we psychoanalysts must stand upon the earth, no matter how slimy or muddy or fog-bound it may be."[39]

We have seen something of the man and his mind and some indication of the impact he made on America. Tillich is the author of a number of smaller, specific works, but those who want to begin to master his thought must face up to his *Systematic Theology*, a difficult, complex, abstract work written in the language of traditional and existentialist metaphysics, but the most definitive statement of his ideas and insights. The following chapters, based on the three volumes of the *Systematic Theology*, will provide some direction in comprehending Tillich's thought and discovering his promise.

II.
The Theologian in the
Boundary Situation:
Philosophy and Theology

All his life Paul Tillich considered himself to be on the boundary between theology and philosophy, from his boyhood when in the dusty corner of a minister's bookshelf he found (and read) Schwegler's *History of Philosophy* to his advanced years when he constructed his theological system on the relationship of the two modes of thought. Thus, that which awaits examination is a philosophical theology, "the method and the structure of a theological system written from an apologetic point of view and carried through in a continuous correlation with philosophy."[1]

HOW A THEOLOGIAN BEGINS

This theologian begins with a definition. His definition is that theology, as a function of the Christian church, is the systematic interpretation of the contents of the Christian faith for modern men. A theological system serves two basic needs: the statement of the truth of the Christian message and the interpretation of this truth for every new generation. Hence, it alternates between two poles—the pole of eternal truth and that of the temporal situation—and the proper aim of every theological system is to balance these two needs perfectly.[2] This is what Paul Tillich has tried to do.

Since theology is a work of the church, it does not exist outside the community of those who affirm that Jesus is the Christ. Theology is not research, history, analysis, or just general reflection. Theology expresses the faith of the church in a methodical way. It follows that the theologian operates inside a rather narrow circle. Both he and the philosopher are motivated by a general "mystical a priori" ("an immediate experience of something ultimate in value and being of which one can become intuitively aware"). The mystical a priori might well be found in such concepts as "being itself" (the Medieval Scholastics), "universal substance" (Spinoza) or "cosmic person" (E. S. Brightman). The theologian, however, adds to this general experience of something ultimate the specific criterion of the Christian message; he works at being consciously and intentionally specific and concrete. According to Tillich, he enters the theological circle with a concrete commitment.[3]

1. Faith and Ultimate Concern

Yet once the theologian is inside the circle, a strange and serious problem raises its hand to be recognized. The theologian is in the faith situation; he has made an existential decision—but no one, not even the most famous of theologians, can claim to be wholly in the faith situation, inasmuch as faith includes doubt! In *Dynamics of Faith* Tillich explains that when talking about faith, he has more in mind than simply believing that something is true. Faith must be understood as being ultimately concerned, which then means that doubt is a necessary element in faith. No, it is not "scientific doubt," doubt about facts or conclusions; nor is it "skeptical doubt," an attitude of actually rejecting every certainty and one that leads to despair or cynicism. Doubt as a necessary element in faith is "existential doubt," the doubt of the person who is ultimately concerned about a concrete content. Existential doubt is awareness of the element of insecurity in each and every existential truth. Faith that carries along with it the doubt about itself must perforce include courage. It is not that faith is courage as such, but any act in which courage accepts risk surely, in Tillich's estimation, belongs to the dynamics of faith.[4] Doubt is a basic ingredient of faith, even for the theologian inside the circle of commitment.

So much for doubt. But what of faith itself? "Faith is the state of being ultimately concerned: the dynamics of faith are the dynamics of man's ultimate concern."[5] Ultimate concern is Tillich's abstract translation of the great commandment: "You shall love the Lord your God with all your heart, and with all your soul, and with all your mind, and with all your strength" (Mark 12:30, RSV). Because the concept of ultimate concern is so essential to Tillich's thought, further elaboration is in order.

First, religious concern is *ultimate* in that it excludes every other concern from the state of ultimacy. All other concerns—physical, social, political, intellectual, for example—are preliminary and conditional, while ultimate concern is unconditional and total. Ultimacy demands total surrender and promises total fulfillment. Detached objectivity is no longer possible. To be ultimately concerned is to be utterly committed with a wholehearted and single-minded seriousness—a life-and-death matter, in other words. This is what Tillich means when he notes that concern points to the "existential" character of religious experience.[6]

Ultimate concern is the price of admission to the theological circle, but Tillich wants to make things even clearer, by setting up two formal criteria of theology. The first is: *"The object of theology is what concerns us ultimately. Only those propositions are theological which deal with their object insofar as it can become a matter of ultimate concern for us."*[7] This statement serves as a reminder to the theologian that he must not try to be an expert in matters of partial or preliminary concern (science, medicine, politics, etc.); likewise, the experts in these matters should not claim to be experts in theology. It would seem that he is saying there are no possibilities of mutual encounter between ultimate concern and preliminary concerns. It would be wrong to think this, for there are three possible relations of preliminary concerns to ultimate concern: (1) Mutual indifference, wherein ultimate concern is placed beside other concerns and in the process loses its ultimacy. (2) Idolatry, whenever a preliminary concern is raised to ultimacy. Elevating something finite to the level of infinite significance creates the demonic as it invades the territory of the truly ultimate (Tillich's favorite example of this form of idolatry is twentieth-century nationalism, wherein everything is centered in the nation as god). (3) The right way, the "one in which a preliminary concern becomes the vehicle of the ultimate concern without claiming ultimacy for itself."[8] When this happens, the infinite becomes real and the ultimate concern can be actualized. Also, when it happens this way, the finite concern is not elevated to ultimate status—nor does it rest indifferently alongside the ultimate. This is why Tillich can attest to the fact that paintings, music, historical or psychological insights, social ideas, political programs, what have you—all can become "objects of theology," not from anything inherent in their own structure, but from the point of view of their ability to express some aspects of that which concerns us ultimately.[9]

What does concern us ultimately? In answer, Tillich does not use the word "God" at this point; instead, he presents the second formal criterion of theology: *"Our ultimate concern is that which determines our being or not-being. Only those statements are theological which deal with their object insofar as it can become a matter of being or not-being for us."*[10] The second criterion is not directed to any special content, symbol or doctrine. It speaks of "being," although the word used here does not refer to mere existence in time and space. The term "being" refers to the whole of human reality—the structure and meaning and aim of existence. In this sense man *is* ultimately concerned about his meaning and very being. The old phrase "To be or not to be" *is*, beyond all question, a matter of ultimate, total and infinite concern. The second criterion of theology does not exhaust Tillich's ideas on being. The whole second part of volume one of his *Systematic Theology* is entitled, "Being and God." More will be said about being in Chapter III.

2. Sources, Experience, Norm

The theologian draws his material from three sources: the Bible, church history, and the history of religion and culture. Some mistakenly think that the Bible by itself is sufficient; yet a moment's thought will show that to be received and understood, the Biblical message requires at least some preparation in human religion and culture. Furthermore, the message would never have reached us if it were not for the church's experience of, and participation in, that message. All the same, the Bible does stand as the basic source, if for no other reason than that it is the original document about the events on which the church is founded. Yet "document" should not be read "legal document." The Bible is documentary in character only because it contains the original witness of those who participated in the revealing events. As for Tillich's view of Biblical inspiration, he writes: "The inspiration of the biblical writers is their receptive and creative response to potentially revelatory facts. The inspiration of the writers of the New Testament is their acceptance of Jesus as the Christ, and with him, of the New Being...."[11] Beginning his theology from the side of man, he can declare that there is no revelation unless someone is there to receive it, which means that the act of reception is a part of the event itself. This, in turn, necessitates regarding the Bible as both original event and original document. It can be said that it witnesses to that of which it is a part.

Whenever the systematic theologian uses the Bible as a source, he is using church history as well. Tillich would ask: Is not the formation of the Bible an event within the history of the church? But more explicitly, he adopts a middle position between the two extremes of radical Protestant biblicism and the view of the Catholic Church. Opposing biblicism, he contends that no one can take a mighty leap over two thousand years of church history and instantaneously become contemporaneous with the New Testament authors. Tillich nudges the radical biblicists a little by reminding them that their interpretation of the Bible is dependent on some definite dogmatic developments in the post-Reformation period (one just does not escape church history!).

Opposing the traditional Catholic position, Tillich cannot condone the subjection of theology to the decisions of councils and popes, the consequence of which is the reduction of the Catholic theologians' labors to an exact, polemical interpretation of the church's own doctrinal traditions.

Tillich employs what he calls the "Protestant principle" (the rule that all finite expressions of man's experience of God must finally be denied, or else they will become idolatrous distortions, and that only in their self-denial can they affirm God). He thus feels himself free to make use of all the materials provided by church history without being bound in any way by them.[12]

The third source, a broader one than the Bible and church history, is the history of religion and culture. Again, the theologian cannot escape this source, owing to the fact that his own spiritual life, the way he thinks, his language, and his education are all conditioned by the religious and cultural traditions in which he has grown up. This is a somewhat indirect, unconscious relationship to religion and culture. In more direct fashion, Tillich asserts that the theologian uses religion and culture as his means of expression, battles them whenever they oppose the Christian message, and most of all, composes the existential questions implied in them to which his theology is the answer. From the history of religion and culture comes the source for the subject matter of the first half of each part of Tillich's system.[13]

More study of the method of correlation must be undertaken shortly, but it is sufficient to observe now that this method demands a link between its two parts—existential question and theological answer. That link is human experience. "Experience is the medium through which the sources 'speak' to us, through which we can receive them."[14] One's own subjective experience is excluded as a source for theology. Jesus as the Christ, not something else, is always the basis for Christian theology. What Tillich does view as the function of experience is active participation in the revelatory event, what he calls "experience by participation." Every theologian, every believer, stands in a dynamic relation to truth because of his experience and participation in the power of his theological sources. In short, he does not just coldly and factually analyze his sources. His theological utterances are always informed by the power of his mediating experience.[15]

The sources and the medium of experience are not reliable unless they are brought under the control of a norm.[16] The source material by itself is too broad and variegated while the mediating function of experience by itself is too indefinite. Sources and medium need a norm to serve as a guide if a systematic theology is to be written.

Valid theological norms develop slowly and unconsciously out of the needs of the church in every period of its history. To cite just two examples: In the Reformation period the norm was Luther's justification by faith; in modern liberal Protestantism it was the personal and social ideal represented by the "synoptic" Jesus.

Tillich proposes a norm, not just a private norm for himself, but one that will preserve the same substance that was in the norms of the Reformers and modern liberal theology and yet, at the same time, will be more effective today. He sees the big question now as not being that of a merciful God and the forgiveness of one's sins (Reformation) or the personal religious life and the Christianization of society (modern liberal theology), but rather the question of how the self-estrangement of our existence will be overcome, the question of reconciliation and reunion, of meaning and hope. The answer is given in the Christian message of the "New Being," whose presence is realized in Jesus the Christ and whose power is triumphant over the demonic separations of the old order of reality. Stated emphatically, the most authentic and most currently adequate norm is "the New Being in Jesus as the Christ as our ultimate concern."[17]

Tillich resists making the Bible itself the norm, as many other Protestant theologians have tried to do, on the basis that it is too diverse a collection of religious writings to be a satisfactory norm. A more particular norm is required, one that is derived from the Bible, and yet a norm that will serve in evaluating and interpreting the many books of the Bible. It has already been shown that the norm changes throughout church history. Hence, one must conclude that at any period in time the norm is a principle derived from the Bible in the life of the church. Because it is a truism that the church does not live in a vacuum, the norm is to a greater or lesser degree conditioned by the cultural milieu in which it develops. Further, the norm grows within the medium of collective and individual experience.

To recapitulate, the norm for Tillich's theology is *the New Being in Jesus as the Christ as our ultimate concern.* It is produced in the life of the church, derived from the Bible, conditioned by culture, and made to "come alive" by experience.

PHILOSOPHY AND THEOLOGY

In light of the difficulty of finding a generally accepted definition of philosophy, Tillich offers his own, admittedly a broad one: "That cognitive approach to reality in which reality as such is the object."[18] In this definition philosophy is viewed as the attempt to answer the most general questions about the nature of reality and human existence. Philosophy, in other words, tries to find the universal categories in which being is experienced.

The fundamental philosophical question in Tillich's estimation is: What does it mean to be? Philosophy, at least in the West, has spent a great deal of time investigating the nature and structure of being, the whole of human reality—in short, all that is, as opposed to that which is not. The term for such an investigation is "ontology," literally the study of being (or reality). Ontology, basically, is what philosophy is all about, Tillich argues, and he can summon to his defense a long line of philosophers going back to Plato and Aristotle. Every other philosophical inquiry—indeed, all our thinking—inevitably rests upon assumptions about the nature of being.

This high view of ontology has, of course, been challenged in recent philosophical movements. Logical positivism and linguistic analysis question the ability of traditional ontology to compose a meaningful language. Tillich, who is so concerned to speak to man's present condition, has been accused of not taking sufficient account of these major philosophical currents. Tillich's unworried reply is that he has, and that positivism and analysis in their concentration on semantics have overlooked the relation of signs, symbols and logical operations to reality. Any inquiry into these relations necessarily embraces the structure of being and, consequently, is ontological.

If philosophy is inextricably tied to the question of being, so is theology. The object of theology must have reality or being, or else it would not concern us. But theology has to do with *ultimate* concern. Therefore, the object of theology cannot be just one being among others, it has to be "the *ground* [italics mine] of our being, that which determines our being or not-being, the ultimate and unconditional power of being."[19] Philosophy and theology also converge in the fact that "every creative philosopher is a hidden theologian" because he cannot eliminate from his perspective the question about the ground of his own being, while every theologian, in order to be obedient to the universal *logos* (reason or rational structure), must adopt "an attitude of detachment from his existential situation."[20] Succinctly stated, "The philosopher cannot avoid existential decisions, and the theologian cannot avoid ontological concepts."[21]

There are divergencies. Even though both theology and philosophy work with the question of being, there is a difference between the philosopher and the theologian in the cognitive attitude. The former tries to be objective and detached in his study of being and its structures; the latter is totally involved and committed as he pursues the *meaning* of being for himself and other men. Another divergence is in the different source each has. The philosopher turns to the whole of reality to discover the structure of reality as a whole. There is no specific place to put oneself to discover the structure of being; the place to look is all places. The theologian is much more "particular." His source is not "the universal *logos* but the Logos 'who became flesh,' that is, the *logos* manifesting itself in a particular historical event,"[22] and the agency through which he receives the manifestation of the *logos* is not universal rationality but the church. And there is also the difference in content. The philosophical content is abstract and cosmological, the philosopher, for instance, concerning himself with various kinds of causality, time, and space; the theological content is concrete and soteriological (having a saving or healing character). The theologian deals with causality in relation to the ground of causes and effects, with time in relation to eternity, and with space in relation to man's estrangement.

In spite of the divergencies, the convergence is the primary fact; philosophy and theology both ask the question of being. Ontology is Tillich's first and major philosophical interest. Of course, it is helpful to remember in this connection that the other type of philosophy to which he devotes attention is existentialism. We have already observed the high regard in which Tillich holds existential analysis, and how for him theology and existential philosophy could aid one another. Therefore, we can state that theology relates to philosophy at two points: with ontology over the nature of being and "being-itself" (God) and with existentialism over the issue of human existence.

If the above discussion of the points of relationship between philosophy and theology seems to leave the relationship somewhat imprecise, it is because Tillich himself finds it to be so. He would assert that there is no conflict between the two and yet there is no synthesis either.[23] They are not separated, and they are not identical. Perhaps the truest statement of summation is that basically theology and philosophy are distinct, but in real life they interpenetrate. Perhaps the truest image is that of the person, even Tillich himself, who stands in the boundary situation between theology and philosophy. A boundary separates, yes; but a boundary is also the locus of contact.

REASON AND REVELATION

It is Tillich's thesis that human reason experiences a transition or "fall" from an essential to an existential state just as every other aspect of life does—that it, too, needs "salvation." Reason's salvation is by means of revelation. As Tillich maps out his thesis, there is first a philosophical discussion of the structure and operation of human reason in its essential state, next a description of the conflicts which reason endures in its existential state, and finally the answer; namely, "the reintegration of reason."

1. Essential Reason

To commence with a negative definition of "reason," Tillich is not primarily interested in technical reason, which is the capacity for reasoning or thinking analytically or systematically. "Reason" in the technical sense decides on the means to reach the ends which originate from somewhere else. This is the kind of reason with which present-day students are familiar, the process of logical argumentation, clarification, and verification. This kind of reasoning, like the proverbial admiral's aide, does have its place, but its place is accompanying and assisting ontological reason. Technical reason is an important instrument, but still an instrument.

The primary concept of reason, then, is the ontological one. Predominant in the classical philosophical tradition from Parmenides onward, it is "the structure of the mind which enables the mind to grasp and to transform reality."[24] Tillich would want his readers to understand that there is a rational quality to everything, from the mind of the individual to the whole of the universe. He makes extensive use of the term *"logos"* to indicate the rational structure in which both mind and reality participate. The significance of *logos* for ontological reason is that, in general, *logos* is synonymous with ontological reason, since the latter has been defined as the structure of the mind which enables it to grasp and to transform reality. Hence, it is with reason in the large sense—with ontological reason— that Tillich occupies himself.

Within ontological reason there is both a subjective and an objective side. Remembering that reality has a *logos* character, one can say that subjective reason is the enabling quality of the mind by which it grasps and shapes reality, while objective reason is the rational structure of reality which the mind can grasp and according to which it can shape reality.[25] This is Tillich's way of explaining that there is a correspondence between the subjective reason in the mind of the person and the objective reason in the whole of reality in the universe. But this is not all.

Reason in both its subjective and objective structures illumines something which is present in these structures but which transcends them in power and meaning. This is clearly not another kind of reason to be put alongside ontological and technical reason. It is what lies behind and informs every rational expression. Tillich's name for it: "Depth of reason."[26] It displays a "pointing to" quality. In words reminiscent of Plato, he makes it clear that in the cognitive realm the depth of reason is its quality of pointing to "truth-itself"; in the aesthetic realm it is its quality of pointing to "beauty-itself"; in the legal realm it would be the quality of pointing to "justice-itself," etc. The depth dimension of reason is not any of these per se, but rather the quality of reason pointing to these "essences."

2. Existential Reason

Until now Tillich has been concerned with essential reason, reason united with its depth in its balanced and unified state with no destructive tensions or conflicts present. But this is not existential reason (also termed "actual reason" and "fallen reason"), which is another story. Existential reason knows finiteness, ambiguities, and self-destructive conflicts; the major conflicts are between autonomy and heteronomy, absolutism and relativism, and formalism and emotionalism.[27] Nevertheless, in spite of finiteness, ambiguities, and conflicts, existential reason is not minus the infinite or the unconditioned. In the actual life of reason its basic structure is never totally lost. No matter what, the depth of reason is continually present to actual or fallen reason. If this were not so, says Tillich, mind as well as reality would have been destroyed in the moment of their coming into existence, since life itself is bound up with rational structure. The certainty that in the actual life of reason its basic structure is never completely lost is what makes it possible for reason to "ask for revelation."

Thus far we have seen that reason is subjective (the mind's rational structure) and objective (the rational structure of reality), that "reason in the philosopher grasps the reason in nature."[28] These two qualities cohere in essential reason, even though they do not under the conditions of existence. It has been asserted that actual or fallen reason is not entirely cut off from its depth and the rational structure of being.

The conflicts, like the certainties of death and taxes, are always there in existential reason, and reason shows its incomplete and divided state by asking for revelation out of and through these conflicts. To take one example, Tillich claims that out of the conflict between relativism and absolutism, reason asks for that which can unite the relative and the absolute. "Only that which is absolute and concrete at the same time can overcome this conflict. Only revelation can do it."[29] And it is the same with other conflicts. Although critics have argued with Tillich over the ability of reason to ask for revelation, he concludes the matter in this way: "Reason does not resist revelation. It asks for revelation, for revelation means the reintegration of reason."[30]

3. Revelation

If reason constitutes the question, revelation is the answer. Questions such as, "What is revelation?" and "How does it provide the answer?" must now be given some consideration.[31]

Tillich has defined faith as the state of being ultimately concerned. Revelation, in turn, "is the manifestation of what concerns us ultimately."[32] Revelation is more carefully defined by saying that it is the manifestation of the "mystery" of the "ground of being," coming to us through a "miracle" and received through the "ecstasy" of the mind.

Again, like reason, revelation has two aspects: the subjective and the objective. Tillich believes that there can be no revelation without someone to receive it, so the subjective aspect is the receiving part of the event of revelation. Revelation is then received through the ecstasy of the mind. The objective aspect is the giving part of the revelatory act wherein the mystery takes hold of the subject through a miracle. Some of these terms need further explication.

Tillich contends that a mystery is something which is hidden in a special and extraordinary way, something which would lose its very nature if it lost its mysterious character. Never should "mystery" be ascribed to something which stops being a mystery after it has been revealed. It characterizes a dimension that precedes the ordinary subject-object relationship; mystery accordingly can never be dissolved into ordinary knowledge.

The true mystery appears when "reason is driven beyond itself to its 'ground and abyss,' to that which 'precedes' reason, to the fact that 'being is and nonbeing is not' (Parmenides), to the original fact (*Ur-Tatsache*) that there is *something* and not *nothing*."[33] In brief, the true mystery is the "ground of being" or "being-itself."

Whenever the ultimate question is put, "What does it mean to be?" by implication there is something, and there is the attendant possibility of nothing. So, on the negative side, there is a certain kind of shock that grips the mind when it faces the threat of non-being, the abyss, in everything. On the positive side, "the mystery appears as ground and not only as abyss. It appears as the power of being, conquering non-being. It appears as our ultimate concern."[34]

"Ecstasy" means to stand outside oneself. One's mind transcends its ordinary situation. The Tillichian ecstasy is no mere enthusiastic or emotional experience. Emotions may be involved, but the intellect is, too. Ecstasy is the state of mind in which reason is beyond itself, beyond its subject-object structure, without denying itself.

By now it is obvious that Tillich's concept of revelation excludes any set of teachings or doctrines supernaturally transmitted to men. If revelation is the showing forth of what concerns us ultimately, and if it occurs when "the mind is grasped by the mystery, namely, by the ground of being and meaning,"[35] and if it is received in a condition of ecstasy when reason is elevated beyond itself, then God is not perceived in the ordinary forms of knowledge, and revelation must not be thought of as divinely imparted teachings, doctrines, or information about the world and the events of history.

A miracle or sign event is an occurrence which astounds us and which conveys to us the mystery of being. To define a miracle as an event that contradicts the laws of nature is to cheapen the term and endanger it for theological usage. A genuine miracle is primarily an unusual, shaking, astonishing event which no more destroys or contradicts the rational structure of reality than ecstasy destroys or contradicts the rational structure of the mind. Secondarily, a genuine miracle is an event which points to the mystery of being, expressing its relation to us in a specific way. Lastly, it must be received as a sign-event in an ecstatic experience.[36]

Thus the marks of the revelatory experience are mystery, ecstasy, and miracle. As for the media of revelation, there is nothing which cannot somehow become a bearer of the mystery of being. Everything and everyone participates in the ground and meaning of being, which is why virtually every type of reality is capable of becoming a medium of revelation. Natural objects and events, history, groups, individuals, and, in a singular way, the word—all can be employed as media.[37]

What is given to us in revelation is no new body of facts; there is no increase in our knowledge of nature, history, and man. The insight which comes to us through a miracle and is acquired through ecstasy is perhaps best described as a new awareness of, or a new perspective on, things already known. We get knowledge about the revelation of the mystery of being, not just additional information. What we do already know is clarified and heightened by the discovery of its union with the ultimate. Here, beyond any question, is a key point in Tillich's understanding of revelation: Whatever elicits one's ultimate loyalty, or grasps one as the ultimate in being and meaning, is revelation. Being grasped in this fashion does not negate or deny reason, because reason all alone does not have commerce with ultimates, whether in being or meaning. If reason proceeds toward the unconditional, it does so through ecstasy, by breaking through its normal structures—by means of revelation, in other words. Conflicts may exist within reason itself or perhaps between differing revelations, but never between reason *and* revelation, since reason and revelation oversee different dimensions of reality.[38]

Earlier Tillich proposed a norm for theology: The New Being in Jesus as the Christ as our ultimate concern. This norm must now be brought to bear on the subject of revelation. Tillich declares that the Christian claim is that Jesus as the Christ is the final revelation, meaning the decisive, fulfilling, unsurpassable revelation, the criterion of all other revelations. It is by means of the actual and final revelation of Jesus as the Christ that the reintegration of reason is achieved.

Tillich cuts through the vast problems of New Testament criticism and interpretation to make two telling points about Jesus as the Christ, he who actualizes "abstract principle in the concrete": (1) In spite of Jesus' participation in the ambiguities of human life, he maintains unity with God, the ground of all being. God's presence in him makes him the Christ. Tillich writes, "In all his utterances, words, deeds, and sufferings, he is transparent to that which he represents as the Christ, the divine mystery."[39] (2) He sacrifices everything he could have gained for himself from this unity. Here is a victory over temptation. Jesus' unity with God could have been exploited as an advantage for himself. He resisted. During his life and at his life's end he accepted the cross. This is the acid test of his utter transparency to the ground of being.

The final revelation, the revelatory event of Jesus as the Christ, takes place in a correlation of ecstasy and miracle. He is the miracle of the final revelation, completely showing forth the mystery of the ground of being, and his reception is the ecstasy of the final revelation. His appearance "is the ecstatic moment of human history and, therefore, its center, giving meaning to all possible and actual history. The Kairos . . . which was fulfilled in him is the constellation of final revelation."[40]

Tillich posits the exclusive claim that the final revelation of Jesus as the Christ is universally valid, serving as the criterion of every revelation, every religion, every culture. In Tillich's estimation, nothing less should be declared by Christian theology for the one reason that Jesus as the Christ stands the double test of finality: unqualified unity with the ground of his being and the continuous sacrifice of himself.

CORRELATION

The discussion of reason and revelation has served, among other things, as a case study in Tillich's methodology. Truths from the philosophical tradition and Christian theology encountered one another to the end that the "questions" raised about reason in his analysis were *correlated* with the "answers" of revelation. He himself sums it up this way: "The method of correlation explains the contents of the Christian faith through existential questions and theological answers in mutual interdependence."[41] Revelation's answers have meaning only if correlated with questions relative to our existence as finite creatures. And we can get the ultimate answer to our questions only in revelatory events. Question and answer must intersect and interpenetrate.

Finite man enjoys an essential unity with the infinite, so *he is able* to ask about the infinite to which he belongs. He is simultaneously separated existentially from the infinite, so *he is compelled* to ask about the infinite. The theologian's first step, accordingly, is to be a philosopher and analyze the existential situation. Although he will correlate his findings with theological insights, he works as a philosopher, autonomously, investigating the cultural forms which express human existence: philosophy, literature, psychology, sociology, and so on. Tillich confesses that while the theologian works as a philosopher, he has his eye on the Christian symbols which provide the answer; but still philosophical honesty must be upheld. If something arises out of human existence which is unexpected in light of the theological answer, the answer must be "reformulated." Only reformulated, however, since he is convinced that nothing he sees can change the substance of the answer, inasmuch as this substance is the *logos* of being manifested in Jesus as the Christ.

The second step of the theologian is to make plain that the Christian message truly supplies the answers to the questions implied in human existence. Theology supplies the answers from the sources (Bible, church history, history of religion and culture), through the medium (participatory experience), and under the norm (the New Being in Jesus as the Christ as our ultimate concern). Again Tillich distinguishes between form and content. Theological answers extract their content from revelation; they draw their form from the questions of existence.

There are other theological methods, to be sure, but they are all less than adequate for Tillich's purposes. The supranaturalistic method treats the Christian revelation as a body of truths which has fallen abruptly into the human situation from another world. These truths are the answers, undeniably, but the difficulty is that man cannot receive answers to questions he has never asked. There is another inadequate method, the naturalistic or humanistic. The trouble here is that one never gets beyond question, because the answer is developed out of human existence exclusively. Everything is said *by* man in this method, both question and answer; nothing is said *to* man. The third method to be rejected is the dualistic one, because it tries to design a correlation of sorts, but does it unsuccessfully. Failure is the result of trying to derive answers from natural revelation or from theological truth man can reach through his own efforts, such as constructing arguments for the existence of God. This kind of theological truth is not answer, Tillich asserts, even though it purports to be; it remains question and the dualistic method falls. Tillich knows that there are weaknesses in his own method of correlation; further, he is aware that he has not invented a new method. Indeed, correlation is very likely as old as theology itself.

Tillich's efforts have attracted the attention of both philosophers and theologians. Some approve and others disapprove—occasionally with gusto. The negative appraisals have tended to cancel out each other; that is, some claim that Tillich's theology affects markedly the way in which the philosophical questions are framed, while conversely others say that the answers of Tillich's theology are influenced by the way the philosophical questions are written down. These may be legitimate criticisms, but to concentrate too heavily on either one or both of them may be to miss the valuable interpenetration of the philosophical question with the theological answer that takes place in Tillich's system. To follow this method with him is to see rather soon that the outworkings of the method of correlation are far more profound than might appear at first glance. Tillich's correlation leads to interpenetration on a deep level. What is even more apparent—and this point should not be discarded lightly—is that the method of correlation served him well. It was the best way he knew to fulfill the two basic needs of theology: to state the truth of the Christian message and to interpret this truth for every new generation.

The next few chapters will elaborate in more detail Paul Tillich's systematic theology and correlative method. In all, there are five parts to his three-volume work. Part I, which has already been considered, is about reason and revelation. Part II, "Being and God," makes a study of man's essential nature and of the question involved in man's finiteness. The answer to the question is God. Part III is entitled "Existence and the Christ." Here is presented an analysis of man's existential self-estrangement along with the answer: Christ. Part IV, "Life and the Spirit," covers the actual, not the abstract, life of man, to which is directed the uniting work of the Spirit. Lastly, Part V, "History and the Kingdom of God," opens up the dimension of life called history with its peculiar ambiguities and then moves to a study of the Kingdom of God.

III.
Being and God

The theme for this chapter is expressed in precisely ten words: "God is the answer to the question implied in being."[1]

QUESTION

1. The Ontological Question Again

When one studies the thought of Paul Tillich, it is almost impossible to spend too much time on the topic of being. He was persuaded that modern man had in his very gene structure, as it were, a dominant nominalist strain, a strong inclination to dissolve his world into things. To correct this situation, for it was not exactly a healthy one as Tillich saw it, was not to return to the realist position of the Middle Ages with its claim to the validity of the universals. In his book *Love, Power, and Justice,* Tillich names his goal: "I want you to turn from the naïve nominalism in which the modern world lives ... to something older than both nominalism and realism: to the philosophy which asks the question of being before the split into universal essences and particular contents. ... It is the philosophy which asks the question: What does it mean that something *is*?"[2] Once again, the vital ontological question is confronted. At base, the issue is being and non-being. Having said that, the hardest part lies ahead—to define and discuss these concepts with any final precision. Owing to the fact that they are ultimate in nature, statements about being and non-being will forever be incomplete and inexact. Tillich resorts to what he calls "ontological concepts" in order to further the discussion.[3]

The first ontological concept is the basic ontological structure of self and world.[4] The subject-object structure is viewed as follows:

Selfhood or self-centeredness (not selfishness) belongs to all living things, personal and nonpersonal, and, in terms of analogy, to all individual configurations or wholes even in the inorganic realm. Self-centeredness is as much present in atoms as in animals. Man holds down the top position because he is a fully developed and completely centered self. He is self-conscious. Now to be a self is to be cut off in some way from everything else, able to observe and act upon it, but not cut off totally. Man feels that he belongs to that at which he looks, albeit at the same time he experiences the separation. The basic ontological structure, which implies all others, is the interdependence of ego-self and world.

Self and world comprise a polarity. Both sides are crucial. The self by itself is empty; the world by itself is dead. Such a polarity undergirds the subject-object structure of reason ("subjective reason" is the structured centeredness of the self; "objective reason" is the world as a structured whole), and reason undergirds self and world. "Where there is reason there are a self and a world in interdependence," Tillich states.[5]

Almost as an afterthought, someone might voice the by no means insignificant question: "What precedes the duality of self and world, of subject and object?" Tillich's reply is, "Only revelation can answer this question."[6] Reason has gone just about as far as it can go.

2. Finitude and Anxiety

Another ontological concept of some consequence is that of finitude.[7] It takes us right back to the "shock of non-being," to man's capacity to envisage "beingness" and "nothingness." The most helpful scheme to make intelligible the concept of non-being is to take one's cue from the Greeks and use dialectic. The dialectical concept of non-being intends not a nothingness which has absolutely no relation at all to being (*Ouk on* is the Greek phrase Tillich employs), but a resistance to being, a kind of "not yet which can eventually become being" (*Me on*). The reason for instituting this distinction is to make the point that to take up the problem of finitude is to take up the dialectical problem of non-being. Being, limited by non-being, taking shape as the "not yet" and the "no more" of being, is finitude.[8]

Unlike the animals, man, by the use of his imagination, can transcend his finitude. In fact, he has a power of self-transcendence which is unlimited in scope. To take an example, he knows that he is going to die someday, yet he is aware of the finiteness of death only when he looks beyond the limits of his finite being and can imagine infinity. Man transcends his finitude not by imagining infinity in concrete terms, of course, but as a potential infinity, as an abstract possibility. In passing, it should be noted that Tillich would not have us confuse infinity with being-itself or God. It is only a directing concept, and it does not establish the existence of an infinite being.[9]

Man, by the very reason that he is capable of imagining infinity, becomes acutely aware of his own finitude. To mention the above example again, he knows that he is moving toward death. In more philosophical terms, non-being is experienced as the threat to being, which prepares the way for Tillich to state, "Finitude in awareness is anxiety."[10] Anxiety is an "ontological quality" as basic and pervasive as finitude itself. It is not an effect; it is not derived; it simply is there. It is part of everyone's makeup as a human being. Frequently it is latent and will not be felt at all, but it is still present. It may be the anxiety of fate and death, of emptiness and meaninglessness, or of guilt and condemnation.[11] In any event, this anxiety or *Angst* is not fear. Fear is periodic, caused by specific things—a danger, an enemy, a serious illness—and fear can be overcome by action. Not so anxiety. Fear is psychological; anxiety is ontological, and as such, no amount of action will ever conquer it.[12] At the same time, it is possible to acquire and experience the courage which accepts the anxiety of non-being.

Now it becomes even more understandable why Paul Tillich welcomed the insights of existential philosophy, literature, art, and depth psychology. These areas of study have helped modern man to understand anxiety as the awareness of finitude and to distinguish it from fear, which is related to an object.

3. The Question of God

In the two sections above a relationship has been observed between the question of being and finitude (including anxiety). The next step is to show the relationship of finitude to the question of God. Then it will be possible to show how God is the *answer* to being.

When Tillich raises the question of God along with human finitude, he is chiefly occupied with the so-called arguments for the existence of God.[13] He does not think much of these arguments if by their use one wants to prove that God exists. The trouble is, Tillich asserts, "God does not exist," so there is no need for arguments to prove his existence. On the surface, Tillich would appear to be making a startling, if not shocking, assertion. Probe below the surface and it is not so startling. God, for Tillich, does not connote some *thing* or some *one* who might or might not exist. God is "being-itself" and thus beyond essence and existence. It is as if we degrade God by putting him on the level where we talk about his existence or nonexistence. Tillich's view of God rises far above such a discussion. Indeed, Tillich states firmly, "To argue that God exists is to deny him."[14]

What then of the traditional arguments? Although they serve no good end by arguing from the world to God—in short, deriving God from the world—they do have value because they expose to view the very question of God implied in the finite structure of being. For doing that they can be applauded; for doing more than that—to furnish an answer by deriving God—they must be reprimanded.

ANSWER

1. God as Being

Tillich's basic definition of God, then, is that he is being-itself,[15] not *a* being, not even *a* being above all others. God as being-itself is beyond space and substance, essence and existence. "Being-itself" is a very critical term because it signifies the "power inherent in everything, the power of resisting non-being."[16] Because the category of being is the key one in Tillich's thinking, if God is not made identical with the power of being, if he is not being-itself, then one has to reckon with the problem that he is subordinate to being-itself, much the same way that Zeus was subordinate to fate in Greek religion. But he cannot be subordinate. "God is his own fate; he is 'by himself'; he possesses 'aseity.' "[17] "Being-itself" and "power of being" are two terms for God which Tillich uses. A third, made popular in recent years by Bishop John A. T. Robinson in his *Honest to God*, is "ground of being." Robinson drew from a much-quoted Tillich sermon, "The Depth of Existence."[18] Tillich is obviously impressed by the depth figure, observing in his sermon that most of our life's experiences seem to take place on the surface, and yet on closer inspection the surface gives way to a deeper level, and this new surface to a yet deeper level, and so on. The depth of life is what we seek. He continues:

> The name of this infinite and inexhaustible depth and ground of all being is *God*. That depth is what the word *God* means. And if that word has not much meaning for you, translate it, and speak of the depths of your life, of the source of your being, of your ultimate concern, of what you take seriously without any reservation. . . . For if you know that God means depth, you know much about Him. You cannot then call yourself an atheist or unbeliever.[19]

If we pause to reflect on the depth or ground image, it is natural to think of that which supports and undergirds us. Tillich wants us to grasp that all things that are rest upon being-itself, upon God, as their ground. It sounds as though being-itself is the cause of everything that is or else the substance of everything that is (pantheism). Tillich demurs at such literal usage, allowing only for a symbolic use of the two words to express the underlying aspect of being-itself. Thus, the *ground* of being.[20]

2. Speaking of God Through Symbols

At this juncture some consideration must be given to Tillich's use of symbol. It has already been shown that in the method of correlation, Christian symbols must always be correlated with existential questions; but existential questions are ontological ones, so the answers must be ontological as well. And the only way to express man's ultimate concern is through symbols. Symbolic language alone is capable of unveiling the ultimate. In short, Christian theology presents Christian symbols in ontological terms.

In his book *Dynamics of Faith*, Tillich offers his understanding of symbol by denoting six characteristics:[21] (1) Symbols, in common with signs, point beyond themselves to something else. (2) The difference is that the sign, such as a traffic light, does not participate in the reality of that to which it points, while the symbol does. For example, the flag does participate in the power and dignity of the nation for which it stands, which is why many people regard an attack on the flag somehow to be an attack on the nation itself. (3) The symbol opens up levels of reality which have been closed heretofore.

A painting or a poem reveals areas of reality which cannot be reached through the sciences. (4) The symbol does something to us. It unlocks dimensions and elements within us which correspond to the dimensions and elements of reality. A great play not only gives us a new vision of the human scene, but opens up hidden depths of our own being. (5) Symbols develop out of the individual or collective unconscious; they cannot be produced arbitrarily. (6) They grow when the situation is ripe for them; they die when they can no longer produce a response in the group where they originally found expression. In the case of religious symbols the area of reality which is revealed is infinite being or being-itself, and only symbols can express the character of ultimacy and the nature of faith. Religious symbols, like symbols in general, cannot be killed off by any amount of scientific or historical criticism. They die only when the situation in which they were created exists no more. For instance, the symbol of the Virgin Mary is no longer effective in Protestantism because Protestantism stresses a direct, immediate relationship to God where no mediating power is necessary, and because Protestantism no longer preserves the ascetic ideal which is implied in the glorification of virginity.[22]

The use of religious symbols is universal, with one exception—the statement that God is being-itself. That statement is sufficient in itself. It points to nothing beyond. Since Tillich wishes to avoid an infinite series of symbols forever pointing beyond themselves, he feels that he must commence with a nonsymbolic statement. Then, all subsequent statements about God as God will be symbolic. His intention is to signify by the nonsymbolic statement that God is the ground of the ontological structure of being without becoming in any way subordinate to the structure.

To summarize, the one nonsymbolic statement about God is that he is being-itself. All other statements are symbolic, which means, in part, that every true symbol points beyond itself to something else and that it participates in the reality which it symbolizes. Theology's peculiar responsibility is, by using an ontological framework, to interpret the meaning of religious symbols.

3. God as Living and Personal

We human creatures understand life to be the actuality of being, the process in which the potential becomes actual being.[23] But how can we make such a distinction in God? We cannot. In order to say that he is living, we must eliminate literal or proper language and use symbolic terms instead. And, naturally, ontology provides the material for the symbols which point beyond themselves to the divine life.

Earlier, in his analysis of being, Tillich described man as an individual self, as being dynamic or having vitality, and being free. These are now brought into play by providing the material with which the divine life is symbolized. Man "sees the divine life as personal, dynamic, and free. He cannot see it any other way, for God is man's ultimate concern, and therefore he stands in analogy to that which man himself is."[24] Here Tillich is stating that man must reach into his own being to speak in a meaningful way of the living God; and when he does this, he finds that he is describing God in terms of personality, dynamism and freedom.

Tillich has been sensitive to the criticism that he has presented an understanding of God (as being-itself) which seems lifeless and impersonal. He has answered this charge by calling attention to God as the power of being, best understood as the power of life resisting or negating the threat of non-being. Herein is a dynamic action, not a static one. Moreover, it is clear that God is living, and as such is personal, dynamic, and free.

But to put the matter before us sharply, is there anything more barren and impersonal than being-itself? How can Tillich's God be personal at all? Tillich has confessed that the symbol "personal God" is a confusing one, but it is still absolutely fundamental.[25] The crux of the matter is that God is not a person, though he is not less than personal.

As personal he is both the "absolute individual" and the "absolute participant." God the absolute individual is the ground of everything personal. He possesses the ontological power of personality. He is "the Personal-Itself." God the absolute participant is the principle of participation as well as the principle of individualization. This is Tillich's own symbolic way of saying that God participates in everything that is. He has community with it, and he shares in its density.[26] Therefore, it can be said that man encounters a personal God (but not a divine personal being); it is still more accurate to say that man encounters the ground of everything personal. Man, of necessity, must communicate with God by using personal language, only because man knows no other more profound instrument of communication. But this communication does not proceed from one

[54]

individual personal center (man) to another (God). This, for instance, is not what happens in prayer. The person who prays is not addressing a Person at some great distance. God is already present in the self and in the words of prayer as the one who makes personhood possible.

Personalistic theism which holds God to be a supernatural person is a concept Tillich denies. Perhaps the most forceful statement of his position is found in *The Courage to Be*, where he describes the God above the God of theism:

> Biblical religion as well as Protestant theology are aware of the paradoxical character of this [divine-human] encounter. They are aware that if God encounters man God is neither object nor subject and is therefore above the scheme into which theism has forced him. They are aware that personalism with respect to God is balanced by a transpersonal presence of the divine. They are aware that forgiveness can be accepted only if the power of acceptance is effective in man.... They are aware of the paradoxical character of every prayer, of speaking to somebody to whom you cannot speak because he is not "somebody," of asking somebody of whom you cannot ask anything because he gives or gives not before you ask, of saying "thou" to somebody who is nearer to the I than the I is to itself. Each of these paradoxes drives the religious consciousness toward a God above the God of theism.[27]

Heretofore no mention has been made of the objection that Tillich's concept of God as being-itself is not found in the Bible. The Bible stands as the primary source of theology, and from first page to last it is replete with personalism. Ontology would seem to be a category foreign to the Bible. Tillich's reply to this objection can be found in his *Biblical Religion and the Search for Ultimate Reality*. Admitting that the Bible is marked by personalism and concrete imagery, he tries to show that the Biblical symbol unfailingly pushes on to an ontological question. He presses his argument toward the end of the book where he states without equivocation:

> This means that *being* and *person* are not contradictory concepts. Being includes personal being; it does not deny it. The ground of being is the ground of personal being, not its negation. The ontological question of being creates not a conflict but a necessary basis for any theoretical dealing with the biblical concept of the personal God. If one starts to think about the

meaning of biblical symbols, one is already in the midst of ontological problems.[28]

4. God as Creator

Creation is not a "once upon a time" event. It is a way of expressing the relation between God and the world. It does more. It points to the condition of creatureliness and to its correlate, God's creativity.

God's creativity is not a "necessary" or a "contingent" act; that is to say, nothing is necessary for God in the sense that he is dependent on a higher necessity, and creation does not happen to God as some kind of accidental thing. God is creative just because he is God. Creation is God's freedom and his destiny, and it is identical with his life.

This being so, all three modes of time must be enlisted in symbolizing God's creativity: "God *has* created the world, he *is* creative in the present moment, and he *will* creatively fulfill his *telos*. Therefore, we must speak of originating creation, sustaining creation, and directing creation."[29] In a sentence, "originating creation" means that all things that are have their being in the creative ground of being; the "sustaining creativity of God" means, fundamentally, the preservation of the world, or "the continuity of the structure of reality as the basis for being and acting"; and "directing creation" signifies that which is customarily meant by providence, but which, according to Tillich, is God's directing all things to their *telos* or fulfillment.

5. Beyond Transcendence and Immanence

It may not be too much of an exaggeration to say that supranaturalism[30] is "Public Enemy Number One" for Tillich. Many examples of his opposition to supranaturalism could be supplied, for he never ceased to record his intense dislike of the understanding of God that placed him as a being above the world.[31] It was not merely an erroneous view of God; in Tillich's eyes the supranaturalistic scheme embraced the wrong interpretation of revelation, miracles, creation, and eschatology. His chief complaint was that supranaturalism was dualistic, with the result that a supranatural world was posited alongside or above the natural world, God became a transcendent object, creation was a distinct act at the beginning of time, and the consummation was simply a future state of affairs.[32]

On the other hand, Tillich is also determined to avoid what might be called "Public Enemy Number Two," naturalism or pantheism. He charges that naturalism has overlooked a decisive element in the experience of the holy; that is, that there is a distance between finite man and the holy in its several manifestations. In such a system authentic transcendence in God disappears, and "God" becomes interchangeable with "universe." Likewise, Tillich quickly dissociates himself from pantheism, the true meaning of which is that God is universal essence, having ceased to be the transcendent ground of finite being. The consequence of pantheism is bondage—for God and for finite things. God has injected all his creative power into finite forms, so he is bound to these forms; since God is the essence or substance of everything, there is no freedom in the finite world either. Pantheism, as well as naturalism, must be disowned.

Tillich has gone beyond these two understandings of transcendence and immanence to offer a third approach to the divine reality. In a sense, he has put transcendence and immanence together in a new combination which, for want of a better term, might be labeled "the self-transcending quality of the finite." From the standpoint of the finite world, it can be said that it does not stand as independent, self-sufficient reality. Rather, it points beyond itself; it is self-transcendent.

From the standpoint of God, he, as the ground of being, infinitely transcends that of which he is the ground. Hard as it may be to comprehend, Tillich can say that God stands *for* the world (which means that he is the ground of all things that are), and yet he stands *against* the world (which means that he transcends everything that has being). God and world experience a mutual freedom from each other—and for each other! "Only in this sense," Tillich concedes, "can we speak of 'transcendent' with respect to the relation of God and the world."[33]

Paul Tillich's faithfulness to the truth compels him to establish God at the hub of the cosmos, at the very center of human experience as the power or source for all man's life and thought. As human *beings*, we function within the structure of being, and we depend every moment of our lives on him who is the power of being. God as being-itself is the power which enables the finite to be taken up into the infinite, anxiety into courage, and death into life.

IV.
Existence and the Christ

Paul Tillich once preached a sermon called "The New Being," in which he said that if he were asked to sum up the Christian message for our time, he would say, with the Apostle Paul, it is the message of a "new creation." "The Christ, the Messiah, the selected and anointed one is He who brings the new state of things."[1] He is the one who takes the corrupted, distorted, and almost destroyed old order and transforms it into a new order. With these words Tillich was underscoring the significance of Jesus for Christian theology and for his own system. He begins, however, with the question of man's existential estrangement and then progresses to the description of the New Being in Jesus as the Christ, he who is the true norm of theology and the final revelation.

QUESTION

1. To Exist

Here the discussion does not revolve around being and non-being but around existence and essence.

Fundamentally, "to exist" means "to stand out" of something, but the metaphor also includes "to stand in," just as the very bright student stands out of his class while as a member of it he stands in it. Existence is a mixture of being and non-being (one stands both in and out of non-being) and of actuality and potentiality (one also stands in and out of potentiality).[2]

Tillich reflects this understanding of existence when he analyzes the modern movement of existentialism. Modern existentialists share one central thought: that man's real-life situation is a state of estrangement from his essential nature.[3] Reconciliation, true human-ity, peace, belong to man's essential state, whereas man's existence

[58]

knows estrangement, dehumanization, and conflicts. Existentialism is an analysis of the human predicament.

2. To Fall[4]

Whenever the Christian comes across a reference to "the Fall," he thinks of Adam's Fall in the Book of Genesis. In this he is only partly correct, Tillich explains, because the Fall is a universally applicable symbol. The Genesis Fall should not be read historically or literally. In its symbolic and universal application it indicates the transition from essence to existence. Indeed, according to Tillich, "it is the profoundest and richest expression of man's awareness of his existential estrangement and provides the scheme in which the transition from essence to existence can be treated."[5]

Man's Fall, as exemplified in Genesis, is possible because of his freedom, which is such that he can contradict himself and his essential nature. His is not a carefree freedom, but rather an "anxious" freedom, since anxiety belongs to finitude. Two factors set up the transition from essence to existence: God's prohibitive command and man's anxious freedom. But man has not yet sinned; he is still in the psychological state of "dreaming innocence," a state, however, that is not perfection. Temptation is not only possible; it is unavoidable because the state of dreaming innocence is uncontested and undecided. Man is caught. There is the desire to experience his freedom, yet there is the demand to keep intact his dreaming innocence. Of course, his decision to actualize his freedom terminates the state of his innocence. The act of disobedience is symbolic of the estrangement which accompanies the actualization of freedom and independence. Concomitant with the realization of freedom is the appearance of self-awareness, figuratively seen in Adam and Eve's realization of their nakedness. The positive aspect of experiencing freedom and self-awareness is offset by the realization of a feeling of guilt and the fear of death. In Tillich's words, "Existence is rooted both in ethical freedom and in tragic density."[6]

3. To Sin[7]

What are the results of the Fall? Tillich's answer: "The state of existence is the state of estrangement. Man is estranged from the ground of his being, from other beings, and from himself. The transition from essence to existence results in personal guilt and universal tragedy."[8]

In this context sin is viewed as separation of man and God and is reiterated in the Bible from Adam and Eve's expulsion from the Garden of Eden to Paul's description of man's evil in the first chapter of Romans. The name Tillich adopts for this separation is "estrangement." The term itself is not Biblical, but the experience it describes is a familiar one.

One thing to notice about estrangement is that it means a splitting apart of that which was formerly united. Separation presupposes a prior unity. If man is now alienated from God, he was once united with him, as the Adam and Eve story teaches. Another dimension of estrangement is revealed when this separation is seen to exist within a person. Man is separated from his true self, and yet he cannot be completely separated, even if he is hostile to it. "One belongs essentially to that from which one is estranged."[9]

Most of the time Tillich presumes sin to be the equivalent of estrangement. There is one small difference. Sin goes beyond estrangement in being the *willful* act of turning away from that to which one belongs. It sets forth the personal nature of estrangement and the personal freedom and guilt, as over against the tragic and universal side of estrangement. Sin is a more personal and specific notion, estrangement a broader one in application.

Tillich fills in the outlines of the picture of man's estranged existence with three "marks of man's estrangement": unbelief, *hubris,* and concupiscence. Unbelief is the act of man's turning away from God, *hubris* is man's self-elevation to the place of the divine, and concupiscence is the unrestricted desire to seize the whole of reality and pull it into oneself. Each of these marks receives ample treatment in Tillich's hands.[10]

Lastly, to return to Adam for a moment, we are asked to see in him the essential man who symbolizes the transition from essence to existence. Original sin is neither more nor less than the universal destiny of estrangement which concerns every man. This is the universal fact of sin which precedes the individual sinful act. Turn it around and it reads, "Sin as an individual act actualizes the universal fact of estrangement."[11]

Perhaps now it can be stated this way. In its essential state man's finite life is continually in union with the ground of being. Man is with God. This is where man ought to be; this is his essence. The one thing absent is freedom. Realizing freedom involves the transition from essence to existence, the movement from union with the divine life to estrangement, but estrangement is indispensable if freedom is to be actualized. So man sins. If sin is separation from God, from others, and from one's true nature, salvation is the overcoming of separation in its several forms. It is reconciliation. The question then becomes, How is reconciliation effected?

4. To Seek for the New Being

It is a fact that man by himself is incapable of breaking out of his existential estrangement to achieve reunion with God. In several terse sentences Tillich formulates the issue:

> Man, in relation to God, cannot do anything without him. He must receive in order to act. New being precedes new acting. The tree produces the fruits, not the fruits the tree. . . . Attempts to overcome estrangement within the power of one's estranged existence lead to hard toil and tragic failure. They are without joy.[12]

History records all "sizes and shapes" of self-salvation: legalistic, ascetic, mystical, sacramental, doctrinal, and emotional.[13] Man has tried them all, to no avail. The ways of self-salvation are futile, for man cannot eliminate sin or overcome estrangement and be reconciled by means of his own moral muscle.

This is where the quest for the New Being begins to have meaning.[14] In seeking and trying the ways of self-salvation and finding them deficient, men have come to see the need for a New Being. This quest is universal because the human existential predicament is universal. It appears in autonomous cultures as well as in religions, in two types: a nonhistorical type, in which the New Being is sought above and beyond history; and a historical type, in which the New Being is the fact of a transformed reality, the transformation happening in history through a unique and irreversible process. Tillich insists that the claim of Christianity to universality is based on its belief that the various forms the quest for the New Being has taken are resolved in Jesus as the Christ.

Man cannot save himself; he cannot perform the work of reconciliation. The only way this can be done is for the divine life to enter into estranged existence. Christianity claims that this very thing took place in the life of Jesus the Christ. He is the final revelation, the ultimate bearer to men of that New Being which they desire so strongly, the one who transforms estranged existence, reuniting God and man, man and his world, and man with himself.

ANSWER

The careful reader will have noticed that the name "Jesus Christ" has not appeared in just that form on these pages as Tillich's thought has unfolded. The reason is that Tillich never writes the name this way; and he does not do it, he says, because the birth of Christianity came not with the birth of the man Jesus but at the moment one of his followers felt compelled to say, "You are the Christ." There are two sides to the event on which Christianity is based: the fact of Jesus of Nazareth and the reception of this fact by those who acknowledged him to be the Christ. This distinction is blurred in writing the name as "Jesus Christ"; the proper phrase should be "Jesus who is the Christ" or the equivalent.[15]

1. Evidence

Introducing the distinction between the fact of Jesus and the *reception* of the fact raises the question of where and how we get our information about Jesus who is the Christ. From the number of pages devoted to the question of the historical Jesus in *Systematic Theology*, it is obvious that Tillich was impressed by the earnest efforts of several generations of Biblical scholars to get behind the Gospels to discover the true Jesus.[16] The difficulty, of course, is that the Gospels are chiefly reports of faith and not of historical fact. Tillich concludes, after carefully investigating the results of these scholars' research, that the "quest for the historical Jesus"[17] is doomed to failure. It is just not possible to get behind the Gospels to find the real Jesus. All we have is a Biblical *picture* of Jesus as the Christ, and we will have to be satisfied with that. It would be foolhardy to anticipate anything more.

It would also be foolhardy to fret about what might seem to be the deleterious results of rigorous historical research. In the extreme, historical research might even come to the decision that Jesus never lived. What then? In Tillich's judgment such a conclusion would not be destructive in its effects, because nothing can be destroyed that is guaranteed by the experience of faith! And what can faith guarantee? Faith is able to guarantee only its own foundation, the appearance of the reality that produced the faith; that is, "the New Being, who conquers existential estrangement and thereby makes faith possible."[18]

The Biblical picture of Jesus had a creative and transforming effect on those who were grasped by it. It was not a picture concocted in the imaginations of the early Christians. That kind of picture would not have been the New Being; it would have reflected untransformed existence, the old order, and merely the quest, not the reality, of the New Being. Only a vital, dynamic encounter with an authentic life on the part of the early Christians could have created a picture with such overwhelming power.[19] Of course, the actual life had to be there, too; for if there had been no concrete personal life, existential estrangement would not have been overcome and the New Being would again have remained simply a quest. But the believing reception of Jesus as the Christ also must be there; otherwise, Jesus endures predominantly as an important religious and historical personage, not as the manifestation of the New Being.

All this means that Jesus was acclaimed by the members of the early Christian community as the Christ, the Messiah, the bearer of the New Being. In their "ecstatic" experience of the holy, they knew that the divine life had been revealed in their midst and reconciliation had been effected. Members of subsequent Christian communities have found that the Biblical picture of Jesus as the Christ transmits God's presence to them as well. This is the self-guaranteeing aspect of faith, according to Tillich. It means that Christianity does not rise or fall on the accuracy of historical detail in the Gospels. The writers of the Gospels chose their own means of expression to report the impact Jesus' life had on them. After all, men do not express the correlation of miracle and ecstasy centered in the revelatory event of Jesus as the Christ in normal, prosaic, or uniform cadences. Their main purpose was to state the belief that in Jesus a transformed reality has been realized, a new life for men and women has been created.

2. Bearer of the New Being

In the act of encountering the bearer of the New Being, one can fall prey to the same error often made when approaching a large city—mistaking one or more of the suburbs for the city proper. Jesus as the Christ is not the manifestation of the New Being through any special expression of his being, but through the totality of it. To be explicit, he is more than all the wonderful words he spoke, more than all the marvelous deeds he performed, and more than his agonizing sufferings and sacrificial death. His words, deeds, and sufferings are but expressions of the New Being which he makes real to man.[20]

He ushers in the new eon. The distinguishing mark of the old order is estrangement, that separation between essential and existential being. When Jesus as the Christ brings in the New Being, he establishes undistorted essential being within, not exterior to, the conditions of human existence. It is new because the potential character of essential being is actualized and the estranged character of existential being is conquered.[21]

The central figure of Christianity is very much a part of the human scene. The Bible tells us so, putting a remarkable stress on his finitude. Tillich has observed that as a finite being:

> He has to die, and he experiences the anxiety of having to die. . . . Like every man, he experiences the threat of the victory of non-being over being, as, for instance, in the limits of the span of life given to him. As in the case of all finite beings, he experiences the lack of a definite place. From his birth on, he appears strange and homeless in his world. He has bodily, social, and mental insecurity, is subject to want, and is expelled by his nation. In relation to other persons, his finitude is manifest in his loneliness, both in respect to the masses and in respect to his relatives and disciples. He struggles to make them understand, but during his life he never succeeds. . . . At the same time, he is deeply affected by the misery of the masses and of everyone who turns to him. He accepts them, even though he will be rejected by them. . . . In relation to reality as such, including things and persons, he is subject to uncertainty in judgment, risks of error, the limits of power, and the vicissitudes of life.[22]

His participation in finite existence was both *thorough* and *real*! Furthermore, it included an involvement on Jesus' part in the tragic guilt of life. In "locking horns" with the religious leaders of his day and causing them to be guilty, Jesus himself was involved in guilt. In choosing Judas to be a disciple, Jesus was implicated in the guilt of the one who betrayed him. He is ensnared by life's tragic element.

He also met up with genuine temptation. Tillich says directly, "Jesus as the Christ is finite freedom." As such, he perennially faced possibility, and this is temptation. It is correct to say that Jesus resisted temptation, but what is actually being said is that his desire was always within the unity he experienced with God and not outside of him. Jesus resisted letting his desire be changed into distorted concupiscence ("the exploitation of everything through power and pleasure"). Illustration: When Jesus was tempted in the desert, he refused Satan's offer three times. If he had agreed to obtain what he desired by using Satan's methods, he would have been guilty of converting his desire into concupiscence and would have surrendered his messianic quality in the process.[23]

The significant and striking thing about the Biblical picture of Jesus as the Christ is that there are no indications of estrangement between him and God, between him and his world, and between him and himself. He has only finite freedom under the conditions of time and space, yet he is not separated at all from the ground of his being. On account of this, he is able to win the victory over temptation (Item: He resists the desert temptations), and over the two other marks of human estrangement, unbelief (Item: On the cross he cries out to his God who has forsaken him) and *hubris* (Item: At the time Peter first calls him the Christ, while he accepts the title, he announces his coming violent death and warns his hearers not to make public his messianic role).[24] Concupiscence, unbelief, and *hubris* are defeated by the New Being as it is manifested in the life of Jesus as the Christ, but the general negativities of human existence— finitude and anxiety—do remain. Tillich insists that the Biblical picture portrays Jesus the Christ as accepting these and transcending them, though not removing them, in the power of his unity with God.[25]

But now a most troublesome issue arises. Jesus' participation in finite existence is most real at the same time as his unity with God is maintained absolutely. How to account for this? In more traditional language, how can Jesus be truly man and truly God?

The traditional answer to this question was given in A.D. 451 at the Council of Chalcedon. The Chalcedonian creed teaches that the two natures, divinity and humanity, were united in one person without any diminution of the distinctive characteristics of each. Tillich asks two questions about this Christological statement: Was it able to fulfill its purpose of reaffirming the message of Jesus as the Christ against actual distortions? Did it provide a conceptually clear statement of the meaning of the Christian message? He answers the first in the affirmative, the second in the negative.[26]

He does not stand alone among modern theologians in his dislike of the "two natures" concept, his main criticism being that it provides a very static approach to Jesus as the Christ. The two natures "lie beside each other like blocks . . . whose unity cannot be understood at all," he complains. What is needed is a more dynamic picture of Jesus as the Christ.[27]

Nor is he very enthusiastic about the use of the word "incarnation." If its intention is to make known "the paradox that he who transcends the universe appears in it and under its conditions," that is one thing. However, if it suggests a rather literal God-has-become-man, "a mythology of metamorphosis"—and it can very easily, according to Tillich—it must be rejected, since the crucial question is, How does something which becomes something else also remain what it is?[28] Tillich takes with utmost seriousness the conviction that the divine is, and must at all costs remain, divine. It cannot become something else. And he cannot help thinking that in the traditional interpretations of the person of Jesus the Christ this conviction of his is compromised.

What he desires, then, is to devise some expression which in a "dynamic-relational" fashion will make clear that in Jesus as the Christ the eternal unity of God and man has become a reality in historical existence. Rather than try to unite two distinct natures, Tillich proposes an "essential" unity, one that rests back on the eternal or original character of divinity and humanity. His concept of unity must perforce be the reestablishment of the eternal unity between God and man. The doctrine of the two natures ought to be replaced by the concept of "eternal God-man-unity" (or "eternal God-Manhood").[29]

Earlier it was explained that in man's essential state he is united with God, the ground of his being. He is aware of finitude, but the threats and dangers of finitude are continually overcome because of his prior unity with God. Of course, his freedom has not yet been actualized. In the act of his Fall, when his freedom is actualized, the unity man experiences with his ground is broken. Estrangement results. It is in the person of Jesus as the Christ that the estrangement is overcome and the original (eternal, essential) unity is reestablished. This accomplishment comes by means of the full participation of Jesus as the Christ in finite existence (including finite freedom)[30] as he conquers the marks of estrangement, concupis-

cence, unbelief, and *hubris,* and transcends the negativities of existence, his finitude and anxiety. There is no return on his part to some
state of pure essence. Rather, it is the "essentialization" of finite
existence, the actualization of the New Being. Therefore, in Christ
the reconciliation of essence and existence is realized and a new life
is now possible. The new eon has arrived.

3. Cross and Resurrection

If Christ is the one who ushers in the New Being and saves men
and women from existential estrangement and its self-destructive
consequences, it is proper to ask, as Tillich does, In what way is
Jesus the Christ the savior? Or, in what way does the unique event of
Jesus the Christ have significance for every human being and, finally,
for the whole universe?

Two central symbols provide the answer: Cross and Resurrection,
each corresponding to the two basic relations of the Christ to
existential estrangement. The Cross corresponds to his subjection to
existence; the Resurrection, to his conquest of it.[31] And they had better
not be separated! Since they are interdependent symbols, the Cross
becomes the Cross of him who has conquered the death of estrangement, and the Resurrection is the Resurrection of the one who
subjected himself to the death of estrangement. In both cases there is
fact; something took place in human history. That, too, is note-
worthy, because if these events had not taken place within human
existence, Christ could not have entered existence and conquered it.
The difference between the two events is that the Crucifixion took
place in the strong light of historical observation while the Resurrection is shrouded in mystery, the experience of only a few individuals.
Even so, there is enough information surrounding these events to say
that each is an *event* as well as a *symbol.*[32]

Recognizing the mysterious aspect of the Resurrection, one is
prone to ask how it could have occurred. Three theories—the physical,
the spiritual, and the psychological—are scrutinized and set aside before Tillich offers his own: the "restitution theory." It, too, is a
theory, probable but not certain.[33]

Beginning with his explanation, Tillich points out that we must see
what is overcome by the Resurrection. The negativity which is
overcome is that of the disappearance of him whose being is the New
Being. The disciples were bothered on the one hand by the fact that

his disappearance did not ring true with their idea of the bearer of the New Being, and on the other by their strong belief that the power of his being was unquestionably the power of the New Being. Then something unique happened:

> In an ecstatic experience the concrete picture of Jesus of Nazareth became indissolubly united with the reality of the New Being. He is present wherever the New Being is present. Death was not able to push him into the past. ... He "is the Spirit" and we "know him now" only because he is the Spirit. In this way the concrete individual life of the man Jesus of Nazareth is raised above transitoriness into the eternal presence of God as Spirit.[34]

This striking experience which befell the disciples, Paul, and others is also shared by those in every period of time who know indubitably that he is present here and now. This, proclaims Tillich, is the event of the Resurrection.[35]

In one of his sermons, "Destruction of Death," Paul Tillich brought together in one place a number of the themes mentioned above: the interdependence of Cross and Resurrection, the subjection of the Christ to finite existence and his mighty conquest of it, and the present experience of the Resurrection. He declares:

> [Salvation] is based on something Eternity itself has done, something that we can hear and see, in the reality of a mortal man who by his own death has conquered him who has the power of death. ... Do not deceive yourself about the seriousness of death ... by nice arguments for the immortality of the soul. The Christian message is more realistic than those arguments. It knows that we, *really we*, have to die; it is not just a part of us that has to die. And within Christianity there is only one "argument" against death: the forgiveness of sins, and the victory over Him who has the power of death. It speaks of the coming of the Eternal to us, becoming temporal in order to restore our eternity.[36]

4. Salvation

The universal significance of Jesus as the Christ can also be made explicit in the term "salvation" and in such titles as "Mediator" and "Redeemer." Salvation has been understood in a number of ways in Christian history—in traditional Catholicism salvation is from guilt and its consequences in this life and the next; in classical Protestantism salvation is from anxiety-producing law—but Tillich regards it as healing (from *salvus*, "healed"). It addresses itself to man's estranged state, with the particular application of "reuniting that which is estranged, giving a center to what is split, overcoming the split between God and man, man and his world, man and himself."[37]

This being so, salvation from the appearance of Jesus as the Christ does not preclude salvation from other quarters, from those healing processes which occur throughout history. For wherever there is revelation, there is salvation. Revelation is not an increase of knowledge about ultimate things; it is the ecstatic manifestation of the power of being in events, persons, and things. Manifestations of this type have transforming and healing power. They are saving events. It is clear that Tillich believes that all men, not just Christians, participate to some degree in the healing power of the New Being.

But Jesus as the Christ is the final revelation, Tillich has said, so there must be a singular character to the healing through the encounter with the New Being. If he is received as the Savior, it means that he is the ultimate, the final, criterion of every healing and saving process. In him the healing quality is complete and unlimited. Wherever saving power is made manifest, it must be judged by the saving power in Jesus as the Christ.[38]

As Tillich builds his own interpretation of the atonement, he offers several principles which must be the foundation of every doctrine of the atonement,[39] and he draws the distinction between the divine action (objective element) and the human acceptance (subjective element), both of which are requisite for the atoning work to take place. In developing his ideas on the saving event, he notes that there are three aspects or effects: regeneration, justification, and sanctification.[40]

Regeneration, objectively speaking, is the power of the New Being to grasp and draw into itself those who are still in bondage to the old being. Subjectively, it is what happens to the individual—he participates in the power of the new reality and in the process is reborn or transformed. Once transformed, the person experiences the opposites of the marks of estrangement: faith in place of unbelief, surrender in place of *hubris*, love in place of concupiscence.

In the condition of faith, salvation is experienced as justification. Objectively, it is God accepting the unacceptable, accepting as not estranged those who really are estranged. Subjectively, it is man's act whereby he accepts God's saving mercy. Tillich has explained this human experience in a most cogent way in one of his best-known sermons:

> It is as though a voice were saying: "You are accepted. *You are accepted*, accepted by that which is greater than you. . . . Do not try to do anything now; perhaps later you will do much. Do not seek for anything; do not perform anything; do not intend anything. *Simply accept the fact that you are accepted!*"[41]

In many respects regeneration and justification are similar, both setting forth the reunion of what is estranged, but sanctification is different. It is a process which is distinguished from the event in which it is initiated, a process in which the power of the New Being transforms persons and communities. The work of the divine Spirit, who is the actuality of the New Being, is both complex and comprehensive. Tillich saw the divine Spirit active in the individual and in the church, and in the religious and secular realms.

V.
Life and the Spirit

Once more Paul Tillich begins with an examination of the life of man—in this instance the ambiguities of life—to find the kind of questions to which the divine Spirit is presented as the answer. This chapter will be surveying one of the most difficult and complex parts of Tillich's *Systematic Theology*, and it will, therefore, be harder than usual to do justice to all his provocative ideas. Nevertheless, some familiar themes will reappear within the new areas of development.

QUESTION

1. Life as a Multidimensional Unity

The view of life Tillich propounds at this juncture is a mixture of essential and existential elements. Not everything has the potentiality to become actual (pure mathematical forms, for instance), but those essences that do, subject themselves to the conditions of existence (finitude, estrangement, etc.). Life in its essential nature exhibits a unity in the midst of diversity, what Tillich calls "the multidimensional unity of life."[1] The aim is first of all to try to comprehend this unity and the relation of the dimensions and realms of life, and then to analyze the existential ambiguities of all life processes.

Tillich believes that it is in the nature of things for the mind of man to try to discover some uniting principles if he is going to make any sense at all out of the fantastic diversity of life. Man seeks for unity within the diversity. One method many thinkers have followed is to invent a hierarchical order by which all things are arranged on various levels of being; the greater the power of being in any particular thing, the higher level it attains. Tillich would reject this approach because dividing up life in this way destroys its unity and creates a static condition. He would replace "level" with the more dynamic metaphor "dimension." Dimension serves as a better term because it does treat the differences in life adequately, and dimensions can all meet in a point without excluding each other, thus testifying to the unity of life.[2]

Among the dimensions it is possible to delineate the inorganic, the organic, the psychological, and the spiritual. Giving the dimension of spirit its due is one of the great modern needs, according to Tillich. Over the years there has been no little confusion as to what spirit was. Some have held it to be the power of life, the power of animation. Others, especially those influenced by Cartesian and English empiricism, were quite happy to let spirit be thought of as mind or intellect. Such confusion is most unfortunate, for how can there be knowledge of what *Spirit* is if one does not even know what spirit is? Hence, it is not mere happenstance that the symbol "Holy Spirit" has less meaning than formerly in the life of the church today.

Tillich welds the conception of spirit as the power of life to the understanding of spirit as mind or intellect in order to manufacture a workable, present-day definition: Human spirit, he states, is "the unity of power and meaning."[3] Man is that organism in which the dimension of spirit is dominant, so that when spirit as the unity of power and meaning is transferred into the ontological structure of self and world, it includes those cognitive and moral acts in which the personal center sees itself in relation to its environment and then acts upon that environment.[4] The spirit is, in a word, creative life. Tillich adds:

> Neither power alone, nor reason alone, creates the works of art and poetry, of philosophy and politics; the [spirit] creates them individually and universally, powerful and full of reason at the same time. In every great human work we admire the inexhaustible depth of its individual and incomparable character, the power of something which happens once and cannot be repeated. . . .[5]

2. Life and Its Ambiguities[6]

Life should be understood as the actualization of potential being, since in every life process such actualization occurs. But then Tillich begins to think in terms of movement and direction in the life process. The three basic functions in the life process are self-integration, self-creativity, and self-transcendence.[7]

[72]

Self-integration is based on the individual-participation polarity, one of three basic elements of being expressed in polar form, according to Tillich. The self is a structured center, and everything that is has such a center—or, as it were, is an individual. But individualization involves participation. Man, for example, cannot live in a vacuum; as an individual he participates in his world. Self-integration presupposes this individual-participation polarity, and directs that in all dimensions of life there is the movement out of the center toward participation and a return to the center. The movement is circular.

Self-creativity is dependent on the dynamics-form polarity. Everything that is has structure or form—that which makes it what it is—and every form forms something. What is the something? It is dynamics—not something that is, but "something about-to-be," the potentiality of being. In the case of man, dynamics and form appear as the polar structure of vitality and intentionality. Man's vitality or his dynamics rests in his ability to create that which is beyond the given in a directed or intentioned manner. Self-creativity is the principle of growth made functional in the act of producing new centers of life. Life pushes on toward the new, always, and it does this with centeredness, but also by transcending every individual center. Its direction is horizontal.

Self-transcendence rests on the freedom-destiny polarity. Tillich believes that man experiences freedom within a situation or environment, and his particular situation is his destiny. Destiny is not fate, nor is it the opposite of freedom; it is the basis of freedom, establishing its bounds and conditions. Self-transcendence, then, is that function in which life drives beyond itself as finite life, as it pushes "toward the sublime." The direction is vertical.

In and of themselves these three functions of life maintain an undisturbed integrity or unity. But put them under the conditions of existential estrangement and there is trouble. There is pushing and pulling, and the basic unity of the functions is disrupted. Self-integration is then countered by disintegration, self-creativity by destruction, and self-transcendence by profanation. Ambiguity has set in. In truth, Tillich observes, "life at every moment is ambiguous. . . . [It] is neither essential nor existential but ambiguous."[8]

Nevertheless, the dimension of spirit does make a difference when correlated with life's functions. Not that ambiguity is removed; but spirit gives each of these functions a new form of expression. If we look for self-integration under the dimension of the spirit, we find it in the moral act. If we look for self-creativity under the dimension of the spirit, we find it in culture. And if we look for self-transcendence under the dimension of spirit, we find it in religion.

3. The Quest for Unambiguous Life[9]

The root of life's ambiguity is' that in all life processes, in all dimensions and realms, there are both essential and existential elements. It is Tillich's assertion that despite the fact that all created things long for unambiguous fulfillment of life, only man can make conscious the quest for unambiguous life.

> He experiences the ambiguity of life under all dimensions since he participates in all of them, and he experiences them immediately within himself as the ambiguity of the functions of the spirit: of morality, culture, and religion. The quest for unambiguous life arises out of these experiences; this quest is for a life which has reached that toward which it transcends itself.[10]

Religion itself is ambiguous, so by itself it is incapable of satisfying the quest. However, it is able to supply the symbols to represent unambiguous life. There are three of them: Spirit of God, Kingdom of God, and Eternal Life. The latter two symbols will be discussed later. It is the Spirit of God—or, as Tillich prefers, "Spiritual Presence"—which now provides the answer to man's quest for the unambiguous life.

ANSWER

Under the rubric "Spiritual Presence," Tillich confronts some major issues: With all its spots and blemishes how can the church claim to be anything special? Can secular agencies and movements sometimes speak more convincingly for God than the church? In a day when the ecumenical movement continues to include non-Christian religions in its purview, to what extent is the message of the church unique? These are some of the urgent questions to which Tillich furnishes answers.

1. The Spiritual Presence

Tillich has already set forth the proper understanding of ecstasy in connection with revelation. Ecstasy is to stand outside oneself, to be in the state of mind in which reason goes beyond itself, he has said. The same thing with spirit. The human spirit goes beyond itself under the impact of the divine Spirit. Ecstasy describes the state of being grasped by the Spiritual Presence. Plainly, Tillich's phrase "Spiritual Presence" means that the divine Spirit is *in* man's spirit, taking hold of him, *creating unambiguous life.* Man asks the question of unambiguous life; the answer *comes to him* through the creative power of the Spiritual Presence (the human spirit can never force the divine Spirit to enter the human spirit).[11]

Since all of life's ambiguities are anchored in the separation of essential and existential elements of being, the creation of unambiguous life by the divine Spirit reunites these elements in the life process. In the reunion of essential and existential being, ambiguous life acquires a transcendence unachievable by its own power. The covering term is "transcendent union," and it embraces two sides of the ecstatic experience of the Spiritual Presence: *faith*, the experience of being grasped by the transcendent union of unambiguous life; and *love*, the experience of being taken into that transcendent union. Faith needs love; love needs faith, though logically faith comes first. They belong together, constituting one ecstatic experience: "Being grasped by God in faith and adhering to him in love . . . is participation in the transcendent unity of unambiguous life."[12] That, according to Tillich, is divine Spirit meeting human spirit.

2. The Spiritual Community

Tillich veers away from using the word "church" at this time. That term, of necessity, will have to be used when dealing with the ambiguities of religion. When he refers now to "Spiritual Community," he intends a new social condition, the manifestation of unambiguous life created by the divine Spirit. In a nutshell, it is New Being, created by the Spiritual Presence. Spiritual Community does not describe either a perfect social condition or any particular social institution. It is an unambiguous, though fragmentary, creation. It definitely conquers estrangement and ambiguity, but it still appears under the conditions of finitude.[13]

Wherever and whenever men are grasped and held by the Spiritual Presence, Spiritual Community is made real. It takes place, fragmentarily, in many places—within religious groups as well as in so-called secular groups. This is vague and imprecise, and a criterion is needed to enable the Spiritual Community to be identified. Such identification is possible when it can be determined that the Spiritual Community is based on the New Being as it has appeared in the Christ. Tillich explains that even more detailed criteria can be deduced from the story of Pentecost in the second chapter of Acts. Even taking into account the nonhistorical elements in the story, the symbolic meaning is able to provide critical insight as to what the Spiritual Community should look like.[14] A number of points can be listed: (1) The ecstatic character of the creation of the Spiritual Community. (2) The certainty of faith (the disciples' faith was reestablished after Jesus' crucifixion by the Spiritual Presence). (3) The creation of a love expressing itself in mutual service. (4) The creation of unity in which different individuals, nationalities, and traditions were brought together. (5) The creation of universality expressed in the missionary outreach of those who were grasped by the Spiritual Presence, there being no Spiritual Community unless there is an openness to all persons, groups, and things and an urge to take them into itself.

These are the marks of the Spiritual Community, derived from the New Being as it has been manifested in Jesus as the Christ, and expressed symbolically in the New Testament in the image of him as the head and the Spiritual Community as his body.[15]

The Spiritual Community is also latent and manifest. These are not just substitute terms for invisible and visible church as found in some theological writings. They designate, rather, the general over against the specific manifestations of the Spiritual Presence. Tillich has produced the word "latent" for all those communities which know the Spiritual Presence's impact in faith and love but which do not know the transcendent union of unambiguous life made real in the faith and love *of the Christ.* Some examples of the Spiritual Community in its latent form are humanism, Judaism, Islam, and mysticism. The central revelation is absent in the latent community; the latent community, unlike the manifest community, is unable to "actualize a radical self-negation and self-transformation as it is present as reality and symbol in the Cross of Christ."[16] The church is the Spiritual Community in its manifest state, and individual churches can be measured against the criterion of the faith and love of the Christ.

The three functions of life under the spiritual dimension—religion, culture, morality—are united in the unambiguous life of the Spiritual Community. These three functions, previously united in man's essential nature, then disrupted in man's existential state, are now brought together again, though fragmentarily, by the Spiritual Presence in the Spiritual Community as it comes to grips with the ambiguities of life.

The consequence of such a reunion is that religion does not occupy a special niche in the Spiritual Community. In the broad sense of the word, religion informs all of reality. There are no special religious symbols and no special religious functions in the Spiritual Community because every thing, every situation, every function is symbolic of the Spiritual Presence. It is what Tillich will later call "theonomous culture." Thus, he concludes, "the essential relation between religion and culture—that 'culture is the form of religion and religion the substance of culture'—is realized in the Spiritual Community."[17]

In the same manner there is no gap between religion, broadly defined, and morality. The act of faith and the act of obedience to the moral imperative are one act; religious commandments and autonomous morals do not conflict in the Spiritual Community. The motivating power for the moral imperative is not the law but the Spiritual Presence or grace. One obeys not because one has to but because one wants to. To be sure, the unity of religion and morality remains fragmented, just as in the case of religion and culture, since it has temporal and spatial restrictions. Yet the fact remains, morality in the Spiritual Community is governed by grace.[18]

3. The Spiritual Community and the Churches

If the latent Spiritual Community represents the general or universal manifestation of the Spiritual Presence, the Christian churches comprise the manifest Spiritual Community. Tillich avoids the use of Church (capital "C") and in its place inserts Spiritual Community, thus speaking only of Spiritual Community and the churches. He prefers this usage in order that no one will be led to think that there is some kind of invisible church standing alongside the individual, historical churches. The Spiritual Community is the "invisible [or inner] essence of the religious communities"—in New Testament terms, "the body of Christ." Rather than a separate entity alongside other groups, it is a power and a structure inherent and effective in religious communities. Parenthetically, it can be noted that the Spiritual Community is not a future ideal toward which the individual churches strive, nor is it a collection of superholy beings, hierarchies, and saints from all ages, represented on earth by churchly hierarchies and sacraments. Tillich is searching for an "essentialistic" term that points to the power of the essential behind and within the existential, and he believes that he has found it in "Spiritual Community." These two words, better than any others, express the inner *telos* of the churches; that is, the source of all that makes them churches.[19]

Nevertheless, the churches constitute a paradox. While they are involved in the ambiguities of life in general and in the strictly religious life in particular, they also participate in the unambiguous life of the Spiritual Community. This paradox can be expressed cleanly in the theological and the sociological aspect of the churches. Both must be recognized; neither has exclusive validity.[20] As for the sociological aspect:

> Every church is a sociological reality. . . . The sociologists of religion are justified in conducting . . . inquiries in the same way as the sociologists of law, of the arts, and of the sciences. They rightly point to the social stratification within the churches, to the rise and fall of elites, to power struggles and the destructive weapons used in them, to the conflict between freedom and organization, to aristocratic esotericism in contrast to democratic exotericism, and so forth. Seen in this light, the history of the churches is a secular history with all the disintegrating, destructive, and tragic-demonic elements which make historical life as ambiguous as all other life processes.[21]

The other side of the paradox is the theological, which does not elaborate the ambiguities, but which stresses, *within* the ambiguities of the social reality of the churches, the presence of the unambiguous Spiritual Community. It is possible to take the marks of the Spiritual Community (holiness, unity, universality) as the marks of the churches, theologically speaking. Take holiness, for instance:

> The churches are holy because of the holiness of their foundation, the New Being, which is present in them. Their holiness cannot be derived from the holiness of their institutions, doctrines, ritual and devotional activities, or ethical principles; all these are among the ambiguities of religion. Nor can the churches' holiness be derived from the holiness of their members; the churches' members are holy in spite of their actual unholiness, insofar as they want to

belong to the church and have received what the church has received, i.e., the ground on which they are accepted in spite of their unholiness. . . . One could say that a church is holy because it is a community of those who are justified through faith by grace—and the churches do indeed pronounce this message as "good news" to their members. However, this message is also valid for the churches themselves. The churches living in the ambiguities of religion are, at the same time, holy. They are holy because they stand under the negative and the positive judgments of the Cross.[22]

It does not require mature theological reflection to appreciate the sociological-theological paradox of the churches. Even the ordinary layman who recites the words of the Apostles' Creed concerning the holiness, unity, and universality of the church is sufficiently realistic and perceptive to know that the church will never in the future become truly holy, one, and universal. Still, as cognizant as he is of the churches' ambiguities, he is grasped and held by the power of the words in which the unambiguous side of the Spiritual Community is stated.[23]

If this is the paradoxical nature of the churches, what can be said about the churches' specific functions? Three groups of functions can be catalogued.[24] the constitutive, the expanding, and the constructing. The first group points simultaneously to the receiving and mediating actions of a church, including public worship. The expanding functions include missionary, educational, and evangelistic activity. The problem here is to walk the fine line between a "demonic absolutism" which pelts the heads of people with stonelike truths and an "unlimited accommodation" wherein the message's verity disappears and a relativism takes hold. The constructing function uses materials drawn from the several areas of cultural creation for the purpose of giving expression to the Spiritual Community in the churches' life. What Tillich means here is that the churches must not act as political parties, law courts, schools, patrons of artistic productions, etc. The churches can engage in aesthetic or cognitive, personal or communal "construction," if the relation of the Spiritual Presence is manifest in their activity; that is to say, there must be an ecstatic, form-transcending quality in them.[25]

Tillich's interest extends to the individual church member, because the "Spiritual Community is the Community of Spiritual personalities, i.e., of personalities who are grasped by the Spiritual Presence and who are unambiguously, though fragmentarily, determined by it."[26] Just as the Spiritual Community is the essence of the churches, so in the case of the individual, the Spiritual Personality is the essence of every active church member.

Tillich has previously treated the objective side of regeneration, justification, and sanctification. Now he concentrates on the subjective side, the experience of the Spiritual personality as a church member. Further, he makes it quite clear that regeneration is prior to justification. Seen this way, the primary fact of the acceptance of man by God in giving him New Being is brought to the fore. Also, putting regeneration first eliminates the chance that faith itself will become a work, an intellectual act produced by will and emotion. As for justification, Tillich has two recommendations: (1) Luther's justification by faith should be replaced by the formula "justification by grace through faith." (2) "Justification" should be retained in the churches' vocabulary because it is a Biblical word, but the much-to-be-preferred term "acceptance" should replace "justification" in teaching and preaching.[27]

Tillich has even more to say about sanctification. Sanctification is experiencing the New Being as process, a life process based on the experience of regeneration and qualified by the experience of justification. Sanctification signifies actual transformation of one's life as a process under the impact of the Spirit. In the past, different methods have been used to describe this process. Calvin saw law as a firm guide for the individual Christian who is not yet free from "the power of the negative in knowledge and action"; Luther put his reliance on the Spirit itself to lead the person to decisions in which the ambiguity of life is overcome; and the Evangelical-Radical theology of the Reformation period stressed a moral perfectionism in life as proof of one's election. Tillich, mindful that the consequences of the above three methods have been far-reaching, proposes his own concept of life under the Spiritual Presence. This concept has four "increasing" characteristics.[28] First, increasing awareness of the demonic as well as of the divine. Second, increasing freedom from the commandments of the law. Third, increasing relatedness to others and to oneself. Fourth, increasing transcendence, which is to state that there can be no sanctification without a continuous self-transcendence in the direction of the ultimate, or in other words, without participation in the holy. Tillich's emphasis, taken as a whole, is on the increasing consciousness of the action of the divine Spirit.

Once again Tillich may jolt us a bit, this time as we discover him saying that the effectiveness of the Spiritual Presence in the churches and in the lives of individual Christians is measured by its ability to do away with religion as a specific function of the human spirit. He means just that. And he also claims that it is right and proper to reject the term "religion" for Christianity. The coming of the Christ is the amazing transformation of the old state of affairs, not the beginning of a new religion. Tillich proceeds with his explanation:

> Conquest of religion does not mean secularization but rather the closing of the gap between the religious and the secular by removing both through the Spiritual Presence. This is the meaning of faith as the state of being grasped by that which concerns us ultimately and not as a set of beliefs, even if the object of belief is a divine being. This is the meaning of love as reunion of the separated in all dimensions, including that of the spirit. . . .[29]

The expression of the conquest of religion by the Spiritual Presence is yet another version of Tillich's Protestant principle. This principle "contains the divine and human protest against any absolute claim made for a relative reality, even if this claim is made by a Protestant church."[30] The Spiritual Presence excludes any boasting or fanaticism because in the presence of God no absolute claim can be made about one's grasp of God. No person can grasp that by which he is grasped—the Spiritual Presence. Tillich hastens to add that the Protestant principle is not restricted to the Reformation churches (it is Protestant because it protests against the tragic and demonic self-elevation of religion); it transcends every particular church as an expression of the Spiritual Community. It is, finally, the declaration of the victory of the Spirit over religion.[31]

4. Religion and Culture

Tillich has raised the question, "What happens to culture as a whole under the impact of the Spiritual Presence?" His one-word answer is theonomy, although he also characterizes two other types of culture which possess distinctive attitudes toward ultimate reality.[32] In addition to theonomy, there are autonomy and heteronomy.

The presence of the Spirit in culture creates theonomy. A theonomous culture is Spirit-determined and Spirit-directed; Spirit fulfills spirit. The chief quality of a theonomous culture is that it communicates the experience of something ultimate in all its creations. Every cultural creation is rooted in an ultimate concern; each has ultimate significance. The most succinct and precise statement of theonomy is Tillich's oft-repeated statement, "Religion is the substance of culture and culture the form of religion," and a good example of a theonomous culture is the early and high Middle Ages of Western civilization. In a theonomous culture the Spiritual Presence undertakes the conquest of the ambiguities of culture by creating theonomous forms within the culture. The basic ambiguity of subject-object first must be overcome by raising the subject to a sublimity of life that lies beyond both the subject and the object.

This approach can then be used with the other ambiguities of culture. To furnish just one of many examples: The same ambiguity of subject and object is expressed in the technical activity of man. Conflicts appear that are caused by the unlimited possibilities of technical progress and the limits of man's finitude in coping with the results of his productivity.[33] The ambiguity is also evident in substituting means for ends in the culture, so that there is no ultimate end at all. How can the split between subject and object be overcome in the realm of objectification? The answer is by producing objects which can be imbued with subjective qualities and by directing all means toward an ultimate end. It is Tillich's conviction that:

> Under the impact of the Spiritual Presence, even technical processes can become theonomous and the split between the subject and the object of technical activity can be overcome. For the Spirit, no thing is merely a thing. It is a bearer of form and meaning and, therefore, a possible object of *eros*. This is true even of tools, from the most primitive hammer to the most delicate computer.[34]

Similarly, Tillich suggests ways by which other subject-object "splits" in culture can be overcome to reach the theonomous state.

Stirring beneath the surface of every theonomy is autonomy, the condition whereby man, using universal reason, claims to be the source and measure of culture and religion. When for one reason or another theonomy breaks down, autonomy breaks through and asserts itself. Then culture is controlled by the pervasive "attempt to create the forms of personal and social life without reference to something ultimate and unconditional, following only the demands of theoretical and practical rationality."[35] In an autonomous culture man is a "law unto himself." Using his reason and will, he erects his own standards and goals. There is a stress on rationality and analysis, purely historical happenings, technical control, pragmatic considerations, and individual perfection. Religion is not the unifying force in the entire culture; it is rational in its thrust and a matter of personal decision. "In an autonomous culture each area of human interest and activity tends to view itself as self-sufficient and self-governing. Philosophy and science reject theonomous presuppositions; art asserts its independence of religion; morality depends upon utilitarian and pragmatic calculations."[36]

There is always a drive toward autonomy in history, but the more autonomous a culture becomes and the less it is able to draw from the religious tradition of the past, the more it loses its spiritual foundation. As a culture it becomes emptier and more formalistic, and skepticism and cynicism dominate. Tillich designates the periods of the Renaissance and the Enlightenment, as well as the nineteenth century, as autonomous epochs.

The rise of autonomous trends leads to a heteronomous reaction. Heteronomy teaches that man, unable to act according to universal reason, must be subjected to a superior law. A culture is heteronomous when the forms of thought and action are brought under the control of an ecclesiastical religion or a political quasi-religion in opposition to the autonomous use of reason. Heteronomy represents a reactionary turn of affairs in that there is a revolt against an empty autonomy, and in the process religious and political authorities may very will end up suppressing the justifiable demands of truth, freedom, and justice. Needless to say, the heteronomous reaction can never be regarded as satisfactory or desirable. Tillich cites the authoritarian church of the late Middle Ages as an older example of heteronomy, and for a modern example he chooses the Nazi movement, which was a reaction against the empty autonomous European culture of the nineteenth century.

The struggle between autonomy and heteronomy leads to the quest for a new theonomy; and unless a new theonomy is forthcoming, the destructive struggle between autonomy and heteronomy will only continue. Even so, a new theonomy cannot be forced. One simply awaits it expectantly.[37]

The concept of theonomy is a significant one in Tillich's system, and we are better prepared now to see the relation of this concept to Spirit. The divine Spirit grasps and holds man's spirit amidst the ambiguities of life, creating the Spiritual Community (both latent and manifest) and producing unambiguous life. On the cultural level it is this impact of the divine Spirit upon man's spirit which creates theonomous culture. In actual life the experience of unambiguous life is still fragmentary, but the overall effect is the raising of life to a sublime transcendence in which there is essential unity with God, a unity in which estrangement between essence and existence is overcome. Here is the way Paul Tillich sees Spirit answering the question of life.[38]

VI.
History and the
Kingdom of God

Paul Tillich once wrote this way about time and history:

The God of time is the God of history. This means, first of all, that He is the God who acts in history towards a final goal. History has a direction, something new is to be created in it and through it. This goal is described in many different terms: universal blessedness, the victory over the demonic powers represented as imperialistic nations, the coming of the Kingdom of God in history and beyond history, the transformation of the form of this world, and so on. . . . But in all these cases time is directing, creating, something new, a "new creature" as Paul calls it.[1]

An intimation of the importance Tillich attached to a philosophy or theology of history is seen in these statements and in his decision to devote a separate part of his system to the impact of the Spiritual Presence within the historical dimension.

QUESTION

1. Man and History

To the inorganic, organic, psychological, and spiritual dimensions of life we can now add the historical, which envelops all the others and adds a new element. With all the other dimensions, even the spiritual, there is actualization, but only in the historical dimension does fulfillment come. The right way to regard the matter is to see the historical dimension not only as a continuation of the spiritual dimension of life, but also as a movement that presses beyond all relative creations and achievements of man to a time of fulfillment. Tillich agrees that the historical dimension is present in all realms of life, human and nonhuman, but it comes into its own only in human history. He has an equal concern for the destiny of the individual and the final goal of human history.[2]

But now, what can be said of history itself? It is primarily inquiry and report, and only secondarily is it the events inquired about and reported. The observing and thinking subject focuses on certain objective facts, and then attributes meaning to them. In other words, historical consciousness is prior to historical events, transforming mere happening into meaningful event.[3]

Events have *purpose*. Human purposes are not the only, but they are the decisive, factor in a historical event. Events also have an element of *freedom* in them. The transition from one situation to another is in part the result of the exercise of man's freedom. He is not bound to the present situation; he can leave the actual for the sake of the possible. Thirdly, events embody *newness*. Every concrete event is unique and incomparable, according to Tillich. If this sounds too general, he can sharpen his meaning by describing "the production of the new in history as the production of new and unique embodiments of meaning."[4] Lastly, following hard on the previous characteristic, there is the *significance* of the unique historical event. The event represents something larger, something which itself represents the meaning of being. In terms of horizontal direction, an event is a moment within historical movement toward fulfillment and is significant in this way, too.[5]

Therefore, actualized history belongs to man (history is only an anticipated dimension in all nonhuman realms), but not man standing in isolation. The process of self-integration in the dimension of the spirit requires both the personality and the larger community. In the dimension of history "the direct bearers of history are groups rather than individuals, who are only indirect bearers."[6] History-bearing groups must have a centered power which will preserve internal unity and safeguard the group from external danger. Such a group must possess an aim toward which it strives if it is to be a history-bearing group. It is what Tillich calls the group's vocational consciousness. In ancient Rome, for example, this consciousness was based on the superiority of law, that of England on the attempt to subject all peoples to a Christian humanism, that of America on the belief in a new beginning in which the vicissitudes of the Old World are overcome and the democratic missionary task realized, etc. Even these few examples of vocational consciousness indicate that almost any area of life (legal, religious, social, intellectual) is able to form the content of history. Nevertheless, the political is of more importance than others since it is so basic to the group's existence. It is worthy of note that the Biblical symbol used to express the meaning of history is political: "Kingdom of God," not "Life in the Spirit," "economic abundance," or something else.[7]

If it is wrong to claim that individuals as such are the bearers of history, it is equally incorrect to move to the other extreme, reduce the individual's importance, and personify history-bearing groups. Historical groups, Tillich insists firmly, are communities of individuals and not entities with separate personalities that exist alongside or above the persons of whom they are constituted. "The individual is a bearer of history only in relation to a history-bearing group."[8]

2. Time

Time in every dimension never goes backward; it does not repeat itself; it runs forward, ever creating the new. Still, historical time is unique because "there is within it a drive toward an end, unknown, never to be reached in time itself, always intended and ever fleeing. Time runs toward the 'future eternal.' "[9] Historical time, united with the spirit dimension, pushes on toward fulfillment. The aim of history, then, is fulfillment.

Tillich challenges his readers to ponder very carefully what is the true meaning of the beginning and the end of time. The true beginning of time should not be thought of as the creation of the universe. It is "the moment in which existence is experienced as unfulfilled and in which the drive toward fulfillment starts."[10] Likewise, the true end of time is not a final act of consummation which "stops the clock," but rather the aim of history, the fulfilled aim. The best symbol to express this aim? For Tillich it is Eternal Life. What he asks of us is the keen awareness that "the beginning and end of time are qualities which belong to historical time essentially and *in every moment* [italics supplied] ."[11]

In one sense the movement of history is progressive: It is perpetually in motion, and every creative act moves beyond the present, the given. Moreover, it is possible to speak of progress in a quantitative sense in certain areas (technology, science, etc.). But there is no progress in areas of life where individual freedom is decisive—for example, in the moral act, the ethical act, and, in particular, in religion. "Obviously," declares Tillich, "there is no progress in the religious function as such. The state of ultimate concern admits no more of progress than of obsolescence or regression."[12]

3. The Ambiguities of History

Tillich directly relates the ambiguities of history to the three basic functions of the life-process: self-integration, self-creativity, and self-transcendence. Hence, Tillich distinguishes three types of historical ambiguity: (1) Self-integration, manifested in the growth of nation and empire. The will-to-power is a necessary factor in building an empire, and so is the vocational consciousness of a history-bearing group. Sad to say, empire-building is destructive of structure, life, and meaning, and causes untold suffering—Russia and the United States serve as prime examples, he points out in a trenchant comment. Neither of these two great powers has grown strong by the simple will to economic or political power.

> They have risen and become powerful by their vocational consciousness in unity with their natural self-affirmation. But the tragic consequences of their conflict are noticeable in every historical group and every individual human being, and they may become destructive for mankind itself.[13]

(2) Self-creativity, expressed in revolution and reaction. Tillich poses the problem beautifully in terms of the generation gap. In order to break through the given and create the new, the young disregard the old modes and structures. Their revolutionary attacks are unfair, but their unfairness is a necessary by-product of the process to bring on the new. Expectedly, the old react against the unfairness since they do not see how it is possible that they could be stumbling blocks in the way of the new generation. They are all too well aware of the achievements of their own efforts and the greatness of their own creative past.[14]

(3) Self-transcendence, manifested in the form of the demonic. Defined briefly, the demonic is the "self-elevating claim to ultimacy." The demonic is frequently disastrous in its effects in the historical dimension. Because the demonic's favorite locus of operations is the holy, the conflict between different groups which claim ultimacy—

which claim to represent the aim of history itself—frequently reaches an incalculable destructiveness in religious wars and persecutions.[15]

4. The Quest for the Kingdom of God

The ambiguities of life under the historical dimension draw us toward a key question, the question of the meaning of history: "What is the significance of history for the meaning of existence in general? In what way does history influence our ultimate concern?"[16]

One begins to answer this question not by researching it or sitting down to reflect on it, but by full involvement in historical activity, declares Tillich. More accurately, one must belong to and work fully within some historical group in order to gain the universal outlook that unveils the meaning of history. And which group shall it be? Fully realizing that he moves within the theological circle, the Christian chooses the Kingdom of God. Tillich puts the matter this way in an important summary sentence: "In the Christian vocational consciousness, history is affirmed in such a way that the problems implied in the ambiguities of life under the dimension of history are answered through the symbol 'Kingdom of God.' "[17]

He continues by explaining that it was the discontent with alternative interpretations of history that finally induced the Religious Socialists of the early 1920s to attempt so energetically a reinterpretation of the Kingdom of God symbol.

ANSWER

1. What Kind of Kingdom?

The Kingdom of God has a kind of double-barreled action. At the same time as it is manifest (fragmentarily) *in* history, it points *beyond* history to the fulfillment of history; that is, it is both "inner-historical" and "transhistorical." As inner-historical, participating in the dynamics of history, it is operative through the Spiritual Presence; as transhistorical, it is identical with the transcendent reality of Eternal Life. The Kingdom of God is in history, yet all the while it is beyond history.[18]

As for characteristics, the Kingdom of God has four which make it effective as a symbol:[19] (1) It is political, coinciding with the dominance of the political in the dynamics of history. It is also a cosmic symbol where the divine rule signifies a new reality, a transformed heaven and earth. (2) It is social. Implied in this characteristic are the qualities of peace and justice, not the utopian varieties fulfilled on earth. Yet, because the Kingdom is of God, fulfillment of peace and justice is beyond this world. (3) It is personal. It gives eternal meaning to all persons; the transhistorical aim dictates "the fulfillment of humanity in every human individual." (4) It is universal. It is a kingdom of men, but again it goes beyond to incorporate the fulfillment of life under all dimensions (the multidimensional unity of life). In other words, Kingdom embraces both man and nature.

2. Center and Moment

The appearance of the Kingdom in history is not a fixed cataclysmic event. It is more of an ongoing process, and one can speak of revelatory experiences and manifestations of the Kingdom, as Tillich is accustomed to doing. It is impossible to "program" these manifestations in any general manner; what can be done is to specify a concrete revelatory experience of a religious group. This is what Christianity has done in the Christ, whatever else may be said about the ebb and flow of the manifestations of the Kingdom in history. Therefore, "the appearance of Jesus as the Christ [is] the center of history—if history is seen in its self-transcending character."[20]

Here Tillich makes a fine distinction. The metaphor "center" has nothing to do with quantitative measurement; it is no middle point between this much of the past and that much of the future. It does not represent the convergence of the lines of past development under some progressivistic interpretation of history. Center stands for "a moment in history for which everything before and after is both preparation and reception. As such it is both criterion and source of the saving power in history."[21] Of course, there is a progressive element even in Tillich's statement, but only in the sense of moving from immaturity to maturity. Mankind had to mature to a point, seen especially in the Old Testament period, in which the center of history could be seen and recognized as center. And, if it is proper to speak of a "history of preparation," it is just as proper to regard the history of the church as the "history of reception." Let no one think the center with its movement of preparation and reception lies deeply buried in the past! It is going on here and now. It happens again and again wherever the center is received as center. In Tillich's more technical terminology, it is "the transtemporal presence of the Christ in every period."[22]

If the appearance of the Christ is the center of history, by implication the appearance of the Kingdom in history is not a perplexing series of manifestations, each having a relative validity and impact. Tillich contends that:

> In the very term "center" a critique of relativism is expressed. Faith dares to assert its dependence on that event which is the criterion of all revelatory events. Faith has the courage to dare such an extraordinary assertion, and it takes the risk of error. But without this courage and without the risk, it would not be faith.[23]

The event of the appearance of the Christ is the one in which the historical dimension is fully affirmed, and the one in which history veritably becomes aware of itself and its meaning. This can be claimed for no other event, though admittedly such a claim is a matter of a lively faith.

In Chapter I we discovered that early in his career Paul Tillich made use of the term "*kairos*," as he and his compatriots in Religious Socialism after World War I felt they were entering a new period of history. He used it from time to time with good reason in succeeding years, finally including a full discussion of the concept in the last part of his *Systematic Theology*.[24] "*Kairos*" is that Greek New Testament word which means fullness (or fulfillment) of time, or even the right time for something to take place.

By inserting *kairos* at this place in his system, Tillich wishes to highlight that particular moment in history when it has matured sufficiently to be able to receive the breakthrough of the central manifestation of the Kingdom of God. In the New Testament and in Christian theology *kairos* is employed to speak about the coming of the Christ, the center of history.

However, if it is true that the Christ becomes the center of history again and again whenever he is received as such, then it is also true there was not just a single *kairos*. Indeed, *kairos*-experiences occur again and again. "The 'great *kairos*,' the appearance of the center of history, is again and again re-experienced through relative '*kairoi*,' in which the Kingdom of God manifests itself in a particular breakthrough. . . ." Of necessity, all *kairoi* have to be measured against the *kairos*. "*Kairoi* are rare and the great *kairos* is unique," Tillich writes, "but together they determine the dynamics of history in its self-transcendence."[25]

How to recognize a *kairos* when it comes along? Fundamentally, it is a matter of vision, of involved experience in history, not of detached observation. Tillich explains in a pithy comment: "Observation and analysis do not produce the experience of the *kairos*. The prophetic Spirit works creatively without any dependence on argumentation and good will."[26] Are there times when no *kairos* is seen? Yes, for Tillich is not simply equating the *kairos* and the Kingdom of God. The Kingdom and the Spiritual Presence are never absent in any moment of time, but the experience of the Kingdom's presence as determining history is not always given.[27]

From what has been said thus far, it is obvious that the Kingdom of God does not at all belong solely to another world. In this world the churches are the representatives of the Kingdom. As representing the Spiritual Community they take in only persons, but as representing the broader concept of the Kingdom the churches embrace all realms of being, just as the historical dimension embraces all other dimensions. There is one main ramification of this view of the churches' responsibility, and it lies in the multidimensional unity of life and its consequences for "the sacramental manifestation of the holy." Tillich's formula is: "To the degree in which a church emphasizes the sacramental presence of the divine, it draws the realms preceding spirit and history, the inorganic and the organic universe, into itself."[28] In these times of concern for the natural environment Tillich's mandate for the churches is exceedingly relevant: They must stand for *all* dimensions of life, not just the human; for the Kingdom is not just a social symbol—it is a symbol which embraces the whole of reality.[29]

Lastly, a word about the ambiguities of history. The Kingdom of God overcomes the ambiguities as it is realized within the dynamics of history.[30] The historical ambiguity of self-integration (manifested in the growth of empire) is overcome by the proper exercise of political power; the ambiguity of self-creativity (expressed in revolution and reaction) is overcome by positive social growth; and the ambiguity of self-transcendence (manifested in the form of the demonic) is overcome in the continual observance of a healthy tension between the presence and the not-yet-presence of the Kingdom of God. Naturally, as we have seen earlier, these victories within existence are not total, only fragmentary. But that does raise the question of the nonfragmentary side of the Kingdom of God.

3. Eternal Life

Whereas the previous section dealt with the Kingdom within history, the present one views the Kingdom as the end of history.

The English word "end" has the double meaning of "finish" and "aim," and this, according to Tillich, is not an unfortunate development. Someday human history will finish. And yet the end of history also means aim, which is that toward which the temporal process points as its goal. Tillich's absorbing interest is in the end of history in the sense of its inner aim (or *telos*). In this sense, the end or inner aim of history is eternal life.[31]

What Tillich is insisting upon is that the goal of history is no far-off thing, but instead is an immediate existential matter, since we confront the eternal every moment of our lives. The fulfillment of history does not happen on the last day of recorded time; it is always with us, breaking into our temporal order and elevating it to the eternal. Eschatology (the doctrine of last things) does concern itself with what is to occur at the "close of the age"; but even more profoundly, it symbolizes the movement from the temporal to the eternal. As such, it reminds us of the transition from the eternal to the temporal in creation, from essence to existence in the Fall, and from existence to essence in the experience of salvation. In one of his sermons Tillich phrases it in this fashion:

> The two orders, the historical and the eternal, although they can never become the same, are within each other. The historical order is not separated from the eternal order. What is new in the prophets and in Christianity . . . is that the eternal order reveals itself in the historical order.[32]

Human destiny, then, is the elevation of finite life into eternal life. Eternity, for Tillich, is not endless time; it is the transcendence of time.

And so several results can be observed. For one thing, "essentialization"—Tillich's special term for the final eschatological action, that which brings temporal life to fulfillment—takes place. Essentialization is no mere return to essence; it is more than that.

The new which has been actualized in time and space adds something to essential being to create the fulfillment. Viewed another way, this participation in the eternal life depends on a creative synthesis of a person's essential nature with what he or she has made of it in its finite existence. Everything positive is collected and incorporated into the divine life; only the negative and destructive are excluded.

Another difference is seen in Eternal Life. In the fulfilled Kingdom of God, because the ambiguities of life are overcome, there is no longer any need for morality, culture, and religion. Eternal Life is the end of morality, because there is no law where there is essentialization. Eternal Life is the end of culture because the human spirit's creativity becomes the divine Spirit's creativity. Eternal Life is the end of religion because there is no more estrangement of man from the ground of his being. Man is returned to, and now united with, his ground in Eternal Life.[33]

Tillich believes in an ultimate judgment inasmuch as man has a freedom which is different from that of other beings. Man in his estrangement has an awareness, and there is the possibility of his turning against his *telos*, against Eternal Life, even while he aspires to it. The *telos* of a person as an individual is determined by his existential decisions on the basis of the potentialities that come his way. He can waste his opportunities or he can fulfill them, though not totally in either case. Tillich opposes absolute judgments that frequently appear in religious symbolism, contending that absolute judgments over finite beings or events are impossible. He leans toward universalism, the teaching that all beings will finally be saved, insofar as essentialization does stress the despair of having wasted one's potentialities and yet also affirms the elevation of whatever is positive within human existence (even in the most unproductive life) into the eternal. In Tillich's mind, no person is thoroughly good or thoroughly evil. Assume this ambiguity of all human action, put it side by side with the dependence of salvation on the divine grace, and you are either confronted with the doctrine of double predestination or the doctrine of universal essentialization. Tillich loses no time in opting for essentialization.[34]

The only completely satisfactory term to express individual participation in Eternal Life is the highly symbolic phrase "resurrection of the body."[35] This term is to be preferred because it counteracts the dualism of a separate spiritual existence, and the term "body" testifies to the goodness of creation. But to avoid completely the fleshly or materialistic danger, "body" has to be comprehended as

"Spiritual body" (Paul's usage). "A Spiritual body then is a body which expresses the Spiritually transformed total personality of man. ... Resurrection says mainly that the Kingdom of God includes all dimensions of being. The whole personality participates in Eternal Life."[36] Against any suggestion that individuality may be diminished or lost in the resurrection as essentialization, Tillich states quite emphatically, "No." In a fascinating reference to portrait-painting, he claims that an authentic portrait mirrors "essentialization" in artistic anticipation. A good portrait depicts not just one moment in the life of a person, but a condensation of every moment in his life as he has lived through his decisions and experiences. It is not possible to exclude the self-conscious self from Eternal Life.[37]

"Eternal Life is life in the eternal, in God," Tillich writes. This is his cryptic way of asserting that everything temporal comes from the eternal and returns to the eternal. It can be illustrated one way by the preposition "in" in the phrase "in God." One meaning of the "in" is that everything that has being is rooted in the divine ground of being; another meaning is that even under the conditions of existential estrangement, the power of the permanent divine creativity supports the finite; and the third meaning is that all creatures are "in God" in the state of essentialization.[38]

Still another way of illustrating the grand rhythm of life universal from essence to existence to essentialization is not by means of a circle or a straight line, but by a curve, a curve which comes from above, moves down as well as ahead, reaches its deepest point in the "existential now," and returns in an analogous way to that from which it came, going ahead and up simultaneously.[39]

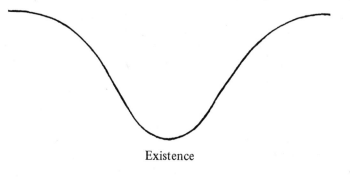

The Eternal (Creation)   The Eternal (Essentialization)

Existence

This curve is valid for temporality as a whole, but it is equally applicable to *every moment of experienced time.* Creation and consummation are not fixed points in time; they go on in every moment. As Tillich himself declares in his sermon called "Salvation":

The New Testament speaks of eternal life, and eternal life is not continuation of life after death. Eternal life is beyond past, present, and future: we come from it, we live in its presence, we return to it. It is never absent—it is the divine life in which we are rooted and in which we are destined to participate in freedom—for God alone has eternity.[40]

VII.
Looking Back and
Looking Forward

One day in 1962 Paul Tillich addressed the representatives of the German Book Trade in Frankfurt, Germany. The occasion was the award of the Book Trade's Peace Prize to Professor Tillich. In his speech, "Frontiers,"[1] Tillich did not let the significance of the occasion pass unnoticed. Three borders had been crossed by the executive committee which had awarded him the prize, he said. They had given the prize to an American, not a German; to one who had served the cause of peace more through intellectual endeavor than political action; and to one who was a theologian rather than a prominent cultural leader.

Paul Tillich, ever the boundary-theologian, in his Frankfurt address pleaded with his hearers "to cross over from what is merely one's own," to transcend themselves, to seek new encounters, to realize new possibilities, to gain new understandings. To be less than human is to remain encased in the habitual, the recognized, the established, he noted.[2]

Again the symbol of the boundary is suggestive as this examination of Tillich's thought is brought to a conclusion. Is it not possible, even desirable, to place ourselves in the boundary situation between briefly looking back over Tillich's accomplishments and then "crossing over" and looking ahead to discover the promise his ideas hold for today and tomorrow? On the one side, critical review; on the other side of the boundary line, promise—new possibilities, new encounters, new understandings.

A wide-ranging and closely-reasoned theological system such as Tillich's is bound to inspire criticism. In article, monograph, and book, parts of as well as the system itself have been analyzed by specialists in theology and philosophy.[3] Not that this is unfortunate or was lamented by Tillich. Statement and counterstatement is the way sound and effective theology is created. Tillich knew this, and for him the *sine qua non* was that his statements be taken seriously. At the beginning of the third volume of his *Systematic Theology* he alluded to Kenneth Hamilton's book *The System and the Gospel*, in which Hamilton sternly criticized Tillich more for his system-building than for specific errors as such (Hamilton: "To see Tillich's system as a whole is to see that it is incompatible with the Christian gospel.").[4] Tillich, patient and unflappable, once more set down his reasons why theologizing in a systematic form was valid for him, admitting at the same time that every theological system was transitory.[5] Meditating on even the smallest problem pushed him to all other problems and to their interrelationships, and thus to the whole, he declared.

Paul Tillich is not easy to understand, partly because of the way he writes, partly because his ideas are at once profound and elusive. There are times when the reader fairly yearns for three consecutive concrete, simply worded sentences that do not contain, or are not built upon, a technical philosophical or theological term. A great deal of the exposition of Tillich's thought in this book has been given over to an explanation of terms and, it is to be hoped, an accurate exposition of his main concepts. No doubt he could have explained some of his ideas more simply, and more illustrations could have been supplied to clarify those ideas, although one has to be cautious in his demands in this regard. A case in point: It may very well be that Tillich has death in mind when he discusses the more abstract "threat of non-being," yet it is just as true that by the use of this phrase he denotes considerably more than just the terminal, physical act of death. He bespeaks a kind of dissolution that threatens all of life and the more general experience of all living beings dying bit by bit every moment of their lives.[6] It would be incorrect, therefore, to conclude in a facile manner that by "non-being" Tillich refers only to death. He is after a more inclusive facet of our existence as human beings, and to do justice to the larger concept a special phrase has to be invented, abstruse though it may appear to be.

Part of the difficulty, of course, is Tillich's dependence on ontological terms and categories, something, incidentally, for which he has been praised as well as condemned. The point is, this is a nonmetaphysical age, and Paul Tillich may be guilty of a misjudgment in his effort to set up the existential question and offer the answer from revelation in ontological terms. Perhaps he is too classical, too much of a Platonist, to fit the modern mood. Does

Tillich's definition, "God is being-itself," *really* strike at the heart of modern man? Furthermore, all too many moderns would think it quite ridiculous if not downright harebrained to say that the most important question one could ask is, "Why is there something and not nothing?" After all, things are and that is that! How silly to go on and ask, "Why is there something?" Thus considered, modern technical man may well regard the ontological question to be utter folly, and any systematic expression of Christianity based on the concept of being to be *ipso facto* extremely suspect at best.

Did not Tillich perceive the temper of secular twentieth-century man? Was he not aware that ontological language would be meaningless to many? Of course. In his more popular writings one finds many more allusions to anxiety, estrangement, ambiguity, fulfillment, courage, and the like, than to such terms as being, non-being, finitude, essence, potentiality and actuality, which fill the pages of his *Systematic Theology*. He knew that ontology was pretty potent stuff for the average man, and that is why in his sermons and speeches he maximized man's existential condition and minimized direct references to ontological categories.

The more Biblically minded person may be irked by ontology for another reason. He may agree that the ontological question is a useless one, but from his standpoint the more important criticism is that Tillich's Christianity sounds like abstract principles as opposed to the personalism and concreteness of the Bible. He may even charge that Tillich makes very little use of the Bible. Biblical references and quotations are at a minimum in Tillich's writings, he may complain.

Tillich's rejoinder is that, in fact, he does take sufficient notice of the Bible. True, he says he has not constructed a theological system on a "historical-critical 'biblical theology,'" but he avers that "its influence is present in every part of the system."[7] And, it should be remembered that he is not at all impervious to the issue of the personalism of the Bible. In the chapter, "Being and God," it was shown how he answers those critics who say that he is ignoring the directness of the Biblical symbols. Biblical symbols always lead on to ontological categories, he contends.

Seen in one way, the whole of the Tillichian theology treats the Biblical symbols sensitively, seriously, and extensively. It would be wrong to say that his theology is non-Biblical. He does honor the Bible. Yet, in another way Tillich has sidestepped an important contemporary problem in theology—the problem of Biblical hermeneutics, or how one goes about interpreting the message of the Bible.

Tillich, in his overriding concern for ontology, has not struggled with the question of the relation between the meaning of the Biblical statements at the time they were written and the meaning of those statements for the twentieth century. One place where this is plainly seen is Tillich's casual attitude toward the historical Jesus, where some would accuse him of supplanting the personal, direct intervention of God with an impersonal principle.

Even so, the main point may not yet have been heard. It is the question of Tillich's method of correlation. It has been impressed on us that throughout, Tillich's theology is apologetic or answering theology, and that answering theology first of all hearkens to the questions of man and then supplies the answers of revelation. Theology, according to Tillich the philosopher-theologian, places human question and divine answer in correlation; such correlation, in his judgment, is practicable only if it is ontological correlation.

But to be the devil's advocate for a moment, what is so sacred about *apologetic* theology and *correlation*? None other than Karl Barth, the other illustrious system-builder of our time, insists strongly that it is erroneous to rely on apologetic theology and correlation. Barth's choice is kerygmatic theology, that theology which stresses the immutable truth of the message relative to the mutable human situation. No correlation is possible. If there is any connection between the human situation and revelation, it exists as the primacy of revelation and the procession of the revelation toward the human situation. It is perhaps best to permit Barth to state his own case, even at some length:

> The problematic nature of [the method of correlation] is obvious. Since Tillich's theological answers are not only taken from the Bible, but with equal emphasis from church history, the history of culture generally, and the history of religion—and above all, since their meaning and placement is dependent upon their relation to philosophical questions—could not these answers be taken as philosophy just as well as (or better than?) they could be taken as theology? Will these theological answers allow themselves to be pressed into this scheme without suffering harm to what in any case is their biblical content? . . . [But] should not the theological answers be considered as more fundamental than the philosophical questions and as essentially superior to them? If they were so considered, then the question and answer would proceed, not from a philosophically understood subject to a "divine" object, but rather from a theologically understood object (as the true Subject)

to the human subject, and thus from Spirit to life, and from the Kingdom of God to history. Such a procedure would not actually destroy the concept of correlation, but would probably apply to it the biblical sense of "covenant." This application, however, is unknown in Tillich.[8]

Barth's comment is a telling one. In the method of correlation the presupposition is that man knows which questions to ask, assumes that they will be correct, and therefore comes into possession of the appropriate answers quite handily. Indeed, there may be a danger lurking in all of this, for more than one critic has claimed that starting with the philosophical question inevitably influences the theological answer. Bluntly speaking, the accusation is that correlation by making philosophy dominant actually distorts the Gospel, thus undermining the theological system. One can appreciate why Tillich advocates the method he does—he strives for a comprehensive statement that will march to the beat of a twentieth-century drum. He wants Christian symbols to relate directly, cogently, vibrantly to man in his present existential situation. His aim is most admirable, but what Tillich has not fully faced is the truth that existential questions can arise from the divine revelation itself as well as from the human situation. Man *can* do more than question. He can also listen, and if he listens attentively the Word can tell him much, including many truths about which he, by himself, may not think to ask. It just may take revelation to show how bad the "bad news" of man's existence is. In a more positive vein,

> Man stands before revelation not simply to play the quizmaster; he stands before it as before the sun, to be cheered and warmed and inspired. . . . Man does more than question; he also exclaims in cries of marvel, of wonder, of awe.[9]

So the kerygmatic element in theology must not be downplayed in the act of extolling the virtues of the method of correlation.

In actuality, the pros and cons of the Barthian kerygmatic and the Tillichian apologetic methods can be discussed endlessly. No doubt the best way out of the predicament is to follow the advice of Professor Edward Dowey of Princeton Theological Seminary, who would have us see that both men are attempting to liberate theology from a narrow outlook or a particular philosophy. Tillich goes to the ontological basis underlying all particular philosophies, and Barth wishes to stay on the kerygmatic plane above all of them. The danger in Tillich is that of being swamped in generalities; in Barth, that of babbling in tongues. "That is to say," Dowey continues, "Tillich's formalized criteria run the risk of being made to contain almost anything, but Barth's wholly material, concrete event of Jesus Christ risks being so particularistically understood as to be discontinuous with life and culture and thus irrelevant."[10]

One other criticism requires attention—that of Jesus as the Christ—although to do justice to what the critics have said would require more space than is available. Some are positively enthusiastic about the concept of the New Being, but negative comments abound.[11] In all probability the criticism made most frequently is that there is a hiatus between the historical Jesus and the universal meaning of the New Being. Notice has already been taken of Tillich's apparent disinterest in the factual, historical life of Jesus. His position is really rather confusing at first blush. On the one hand, he brushes aside any real need for the historical Jesus, at least for faith;[12] on the other hand he does assert that the actual, concrete life had to be present, or else existential estrangement would not have been overcome and the New Being would have remained only a quest. In all of Tillich's Christology one paramount fact stands out: his striving to discover the universal dimension of things. Tillich regards man not in the particular but in the universal sense; that is to say, man in his essential nature and in his existential estrangement. Traditional Christianity has always explicated Peter's confession at Caesarea Philippi as the original witness to the fact that the person Jesus was recognized to be the Messiah of God. Tillich, instead, views the incident as pointing to the eternal truth that a new reality has been manifested in human existence.[13] In Tillich's own words: "Essential God-Manhood has appeared within existence and subjected itself to the conditions of existence without being conquered by them."[14]

Possibly something has been overlooked in the excitement of debate. Tillich knew that man had to live by faith alone. Historical fact about Jesus simply was not a possibility, and so faith had to be uppermost, not certain historical knowledge. Yet we do have a picture of Jesus, Tillich tells us, and this is the significant point. A picture does communicate reality, but it may not supply us with all the facts we would like to have. The historical Jesus we cannot know in accurate detail, but we can know the general picture or image of the man. Details never, but through the Biblical accounts a reliable picture or image of him who was transparent to the ground of his being comes through to us. Tillich did want Jesus to be actual. It was important "that in *one* personal life essential manhood has appeared."[15] We can bank on the historical actuality of the life of Jesus as the Christ. We do possess a picture where it is impossible to have the person. Nels Ferré, who once said that a person had to be a Tillichian or a Christian, sees a clash between Tillich's ontology and his Christian theology, but holds that it is in the person of Jesus as the Christ that he attempted to bring the two together. Ferré writes:

> And yet Tillich wanted Jesus to be actual not only as the key peg of his system, not only as the theological requirement of Incarnation, but also for his larger thinking that pressed theology toward ontology, faith toward knowledge. Only if Jesus was actual could his life be representative and thus universally relevant.[16]

It is to be hoped that these suggestions will help to clarify Tillich's position on the historical reliability of Jesus as the Christ. However, those persons who feel that they must make some kind of informed decision about the New Being by which they have been grasped, and by which the earliest Christian community was grasped, will still find Tillich lacking in his concern about the authenticity of historical detail. According to him, it must be remembered, faith was being grasped by ultimate concern, not acquiring sure and steadfast knowledge upon which man then made his choice.

These are but a few of the problem areas in Tillich's thought. Space does not permit a discussion of Tillich's use of language and symbol, the dialectic between faith and doubt, the concept of religion, and other points which have drawn both interest and critical comment.[17]

Now to some of the more promising facets of Tillich's thought. Because of the comprehensiveness of Tillich's work, it would not be true to him to carve out sections of his thought and hold these up as the ones that contain the promise (as though other sections had none). Unlike so many other modern theologians, his theological style was systematic rather than scattered in essay and monograph. One of Tillich's former students is entirely correct when he says that "everything he touched was really of one piece, without being doctrinaire or losing its dynamics. It is this which accounts for the fact that he could speak with equal ease about Parmenides and Jesus Christ without confusing the two."[18] The most genuine approach will be to suggest certain themes which perhaps are more promising than others, more likely to continue to say a hopeful word to men and women in the years ahead. I say "suggest certain themes" for the reason that it may still be too soon after Tillich's death to state with any assurance what his lasting contributions are. On the other hand, it is not too soon to say that Tillich's influence will be felt for quite some time. He labored hard and long over very fundamental and ongoing questions in Christian theology, but even he had moments when he doubted his lasting significance. In the spring of 1964 when the then "radical theology" began to surface, Tillich remarked to theologian Langdon Gilkey, "Vy, Langdon, am I so soon on ze dust heap of history?" Gilkey, much younger than Tillich, replied, "Don't feel too sorry for yourself—I'm there already too!"[19] Events in the years since 1964 have proved that neither theologian has been relegated to the dustheap!

It is a commonplace now to say that we live in a secular age, that the outlook of ever so many men and women is one which sees no need to resort to transcendent realities of any type to find meaning in this world. They remain satisfied with the observable, the touch-able, the measurable, the finite; they hunger after no ultimate, no infinite, no divinity—even though many of them still follow religious practices in a nominal fashion. Today, more than ever, it would seem that the religious worldview is only one of the options facing a person, and all too few select that option. One feature of our age is the decreasing sense of the reality of God as a supreme being. A related problem is how to speak of God at all in the time of "the eclipse of God," to borrow a phrase from Martin Buber.

Tillich was not blind to the experience of the loss of God. He was sure that some of the despair of the twentieth century stemmed from the loss of God in the nineteenth century, and he tried his best to formulate an understanding of God which would take into account the justifiable present-day protests against a sterile, unimaginative theism. That is why he talked of a God above the God of theism, of a God who as the ground of being stands *for* the world (as the ground) and also *against* the world (as transcendent to everything that has being). This kind of God would be a deity modern man could believe in and worship, since he is at the very center of human experience as the power or source for all of man's life and thought.

It may very well be that in the future very few religious thinkers will follow Tillich slavishly, using the identical terms he used in speaking of God. But surely he has pointed the way. Something in secular man's experience will prompt him to raise a question, perchance many questions, about himself or his world. Even if this modern secular man openly acknowledges himself to be nonreligious, one day he will pose a question of ultimate meaning and will seek for answers. Will it be a question having to do with death, that universal threat to the being of every person? Will it be a question of value, whether this finally is of more worth than that? Will it be a question of security, how even to find any of it in such a chaotic world as ours? Will it be a question of guilt and forgiveness that emerges not necessarily out of a lesson on the Ten Commandments in some childhood Sunday school but out of pure weariness of forever wronging someone else and being wronged in return? Or will it be a question that asks the why of the symmetry of a daisy, the beauty of a friendship, the joy of a wedding, the wonder when a baby is born? These are not "religious" issues per se; they belong to the secular experience of all men and women. But they are the very questions which the Christian Gospel has striven to answer authentically and universally. That is what Christian theology is all about: to recognize the correlation between the low moments and high moments of our day-to-day, this-world experiences and what the Gospel has to say about them. Paul Tillich is telling twentieth-century man that God and language about him are not relevant within a safe, but narrow, circumscribed "religious" territory. God and "God-talk" are centered in a perception of the presence of the divine within the human. That which we call God is seen as real within secular institutions and experiences. Religious symbols, then, have validity as they address themselves to those critical questions that inevitably arise, sometimes quite unexpectedly, out of our mundane existence.[20]

If this is carried one step further, it can be said that theology has the open-ended responsibility of mature reflection on each religious symbol, each theological concept, in order that it may be as lucid and compelling as possible in relation to the question that arose within human existence. Theology concerns itself with ever greater clarification and meaning, once it is acknowledged that the divine is present in the human and that there is an interdependence of human experience and religious symbol. It goes without saying that the answer must be preceded by careful and serious analysis of the questions of life, and it is a truism to say that it is easier to raise questions than answer them. All this means that once we formulate the everyday secular problems of self-acceptance, guilt, contingency, freedom, death, and the like, we can proceed to say what we mean by the message of love, forgiveness, creation, providence, and eternal life. Thus conceived, Christian teachings and beliefs become, at least for Christians, meaningful assertions, since they are correlated with meaningful questions derived from ordinary human experiences.

It has been said that Paul Tillich was rooted too deeply in the classical tradition, a tradition that does not have much to say to men and women any more, especially with his discussion of being. And maybe he was, though clearly his idea of being was not a term for all that is (pantheism) or a static divine reality (deism). But what must always be remembered is that Tillich's involvement with the ontological question was not an outdated idiosyncrasy. It is his way of handling "the religious situation" of our time. The ontological question is *the* question man throws up to reality, expressed in myriad forms. Being and non-being—these are the two great forces that are fundamental to human nature. Tillich felt that he had unveiled the human nature which is not produced by culture but which is the presupposition of culture. In other words, the ontological question is not merely one of human nature but of the nature of culture as well. Finite man in his state of estrangement is the creator of the structures of culture. He lives in a culture. He cannot escape culture. However, no culture can make man over into something other than finite. No culture can create nonanxious man, and for that matter, when men and women cease to ask the ontological question or to distinguish between time and eternity, the finite and the infinite, they are dooming both the individual and the collective life of man. Therefore, there was, and is, an urgency to this question of being which kept Tillich hard at work until the end of his long life. At base, the question of being was to Tillich a life-and-death question for mankind. In another way sociologist Robert N. Bellah has expressed the same urgency.

> In order to break through the literal univocal interpretation of reality that our pseudoscientific secular culture espouses, it is necessary for religion to communicate nonordinary reality that breaks into ordinary reality and exposes its pretensions. When ordinary reality turns into a nightmare, as it increasingly has in modern society, only some transcendental perspective offers any hope.[21]

Bellah is willing to go so far as to say that Tillich's greatest contribution—and the line that is still worth pursuing today—was his active quest for the "dimension of depth" in all social and cultural forms. Bellah's encomium is no mild one: "But for me Paul Tillich is still the great theologian of the century, perhaps because it was through his work that Christian symbols first began to live again for me after my adolescent loss of faith."[22]

Tillich was emphatic. If modern man is not religious, it is because he has lost the depth dimension. But man *is* religious, frequently in demonic ways, but inescapably religious. If contemporary society, dominated by "technical reason," has become religiously calloused, that is the weakness of society and not its strength.

Tillich did not spend his time prophesying the downfall of society. His portrayal of a theonomous culture is creative and provocative, his vision of a time and a condition when ultimate concern infuses the whole web of man's life and thought is significant and hopeful. It may be incorrect, strictly speaking, to speak of "Tillich's call to theonomy," as one writer has,[23] because no cultural condition—autonomy, heteronomy, theonomy—can be consciously constructed. All the same, cultural conditions do not just grow like Topsy either. Tillich's contribution was to survey and analyze the past and in so doing help to create the milieu in which new cultural forms could appear. A theonomy really is not man's to make; it is "more like the miracle of birth than like artisanship"—but it was to Tillich's credit that in his analysis of culture he could indicate trends, concerns, themes which were potent with meaning for the present and the future. In that he could bring to bear the resources of the past upon the present situation, he was a theologian of culture. Theology does not exist in a vacuum; a "theology of culture" is the only kind there is, Tillich contended.

In the period of crisis during and after World War I, Tillich judged conditions to be favorable for the emergence of a time of theonomy through Religious Socialism. Religious Socialism did not materialize. Later, when he came to America, after he struggled with the problem of Christology, Tillich began to sketch the picture of the Christ as the one who was the bearer of the New Being. He thought of the New Being as concretely as possible; it was the coming of the redemptive, creative power in actuality, in the Christ, the center of history. The moment of the coming is the *kairos*. The New Being, therefore, is the involvement of being itself in existence, which means that healing and creative power is operative, that the transforming action is continuous, and that the New Being itself is the essence of history. One of Tillich's leading insights for our time was the New Being, the new creation, the power of reconciliation and renewal which never destroys or replaces creation, but which renovates the old creation to make a new one, brought to reality through the Spirit who dynamically and creatively conquers life's ambiguities. As Christian theologian, Tillich's basic vision is that in the Biblical picture of Jesus as the Christ lies the depth of culture, and that New Being is the ultimate concern of every man and woman.

Finally, there is Tillich's own "promise," what he himself regarded as the future of theology. In 1960, from May to July, Tillich visited Japan and had many conversations with Christian ministers and missionaries and with Buddhist scholars and priests. That this short stay in the Orient made a significant impact on him is not to be doubted. In writing in the "How My Mind Has Changed" series in *The Christian Century* in late 1960, he reaffirmed the importance of participating existentially, entering personally, the situation about which one reflects and makes abstract statements. Then he continued by putting first on the list of such experiences in the years 1950 to 1960 his visit to Japan. "I have felt an immense enrichment of substance ever since my trip," he confessed, and by this he meant not merely a few new insights but "being somehow transformed through participation."[24] Not that he was in any sense converted to some form of Buddhism, but he was drawn right into (for him) new forms of religious life which exemplified an ultimate concern apart from any Christian influence.

Even before he went to Japan, Tillich had held that it was as foolish as it was wrong to divide up the religions of mankind in such a manner that there was one true religion and the remainder were false. Rather, he argued, all religions, including Christianity, must be subjected to the criterion of a faith which transcends every finite symbol of faith and to the criterion of a love which affirms, judges, and receives the other person.[25] This same approach to the religions of the world is exposed to view in Tillich's *Christianity and the Encounter of the World Religions*, the Bampton Lectures at Columbia University for 1962. In that work, in part based on Tillich's visit to Japan, he did not fully develop his conception of the relationship between different religions. He did indicate how he would proceed. Rejecting the "comparative" method, whereby one compares the concept of God, man, etc., in two or more religions, Tillich proposed that the *telos* question be raised with regard to different religions, and in broad strokes he sketched two "telos-formulas" for his readers: "In Christianity the telos of every*one* and everything united in the Kingdom of God; in Buddhism the telos of every*thing* and everyone fulfilled in the Nirvana."[26]

[108]

Also in the same small book he faced squarely three alternatives: In the future should we look for a mixture of religions, for the victory of one religion over all the others, or even for the end of the religious age as such? He answered, resoundingly, "None of these alternatives!"[27] A mixture of religions is to be avoided, since a mixture destroys in each religion the concreteness which gives it its dynamic power. Nor is the victory of one religion a viable option, for the outcome is merely the imposition of one particular religious answer on all other particular answers. And as for the likelihood that the religious age itself has come or will come to an end—well, that will not happen so long as men and women populate the earth, because they will always be raising the question of the meaning of life. What each of us can do, according to Tillich, is to penetrate into the depth of his own religion, because in the depth of every religion a point is reached at which the religion itself loses its importance and that to which it points breaks through all of that religion's particularities, elevating it to a fuller vision of the spiritual presence and to a richer perception of man's existence.[28]

On the evening of October 12, 1965, Paul Tillich delivered his last lecture. He spoke to the attentive audience in Breasted Hall of the University of Chicago on the subject, "The Significance of the History of Religions for the Systematic Theologian." Early the next morning he suffered a serious heart attack, and ten days later he was dead.

Between the time he gave the Bampton Lectures and the last lecture of his life, he had moved to the University of Chicago from Harvard and for two years had conducted a joint seminar with Professor Mircea Eliade on History of Religions and Systematic Theology. Clearly, Tillich's work was entering a new phase. His final lecture describes that phase and lays out the next steps for systematic theology, steps which Tillich himself presumably would have taken had he lived longer.[29]

Those of us who heard him give that lecture recall that he began by picking up an earlier theme. He criticized and rejected two theological positions, that which avows that one's own religion is revelation while other religions are but weak attempts to reach God, and that which he called "a theology without theos," a theology of the secular or the God-is-dead theology. The trouble with both positions is that they are reductionistic in their effort to eliminate everything from the Christian faith except the figure of Jesus. The Neo-orthodox position makes Jesus the only place where revelation can be heard; the secular is devalued. The secular position uses him only as the unique representative of a relevant secular culture; there is no depth dimension to reckon with at all.

The future of theology does not reside in either of these positions, inasmuch as neither does justice to the full reach of mankind's religious experience or to the rich materials in the history of religions.

"My approach is dynamic-typological," Tillich explained,[30] an approach which tries, first of all, to discern the expressions of the Holy within the finite. It is the sacramental basis of all religions—the Holy here and now in spite of its mysterious character. A second and critical element is a final dissatisfaction with all concrete expressions of the Holy. This constitutes the guarantee against the demonization of the sacramental, for all particular religious expressions are relegated to secondary status. One must push beyond these to the Ultimate itself in what Tillich refers to as a "mystical movement." The third element is the ethical or prophetic, the element of "ought to be." This, too, is a critique of the sacramental.

Join together these three special elements and the result is the inner *telos* of all religion. "The Religion of the Concrete Spirit" is Tillich's generic term, since no historical religion can be so designated, although all religions in one way or another manifest the unity of the three elements—sacramental, mystical, ethical. The Religion of the Concrete Spirit is not just a future vision toward which everything pushes. It is to be found wherever the demonic is challenged, in many periods in the history of religions. Actually, Tillich was prone to view the whole history of religions as a struggle for the Religion of the Concrete Spirit, epitomized in the Pauline concept of the Spirit where the ecstatic and the rational aspects are united. For the Christian the appearance of Jesus as the Christ (Christus Victor) provides the victory in this struggle. But there are *kairoi*, the continuation of critical moments in history, which means that the Religion of the Concrete Spirit is actualized now here, now there, though always fragmentarily.

Tillich felt that he had hold of something potentially powerful. He explained that his *Systematic Theology* had been written to counter scientific and philosophical criticism of Christianity and before his lately developed interest in non-Christian religions. By way of suggesting a new kind of theology he declared:

Perhaps we need a longer, more intensive period of interpenetration of systematic theological study and religious historical studies.

Under such circumstances the structure of religious thought might develop in connection with another or different fragmentary manifestation of theonomy or of the Religion of the Concrete Spirit. This is my hope for the future of theology.[31]

Such was the extent of Paul Tillich's ecumenical thrust. No narrow confessionalism marked his labors. He was continually striving for a synthesis, not one based on weak compromise but one which dealt vigorously and honestly with all the elements and forces at hand, those active in the past and in the present, in the churches and in the secular world, in Christianity and in non-Christian religions. But just as interesting is the fact that when he was well into his seventies, his powerful and creative intellect was grappling with new problems and constructing new solutions. Faithful to his own inner *telos* as a theologian, Tillich never finished his theology, as it were. His final lecture is the best example of his own admonition that "a system should be not only a point of arrival but a point of departure as well."

It has frequently been remarked that Tillich established no Tillichian school, no body of disciples who mouth the famous sayings of the master. This is true. Like so many of the world's great teachers, he has disciples only in spirit. For he did not teach a body of truths to be memorized and repeated. He showed us how to ask again and again the deep, penetrating questions of life and how to find the answers to them on that "endless road toward truth." He showed us how contemporary man can be Christian man. If one cannot follow Tillich in some of his analyses or conclusions, nevertheless one must admire him for his intention and for the strength of his faith and intellect in linking religious faith to all aspects of this world's life.

Paul Tillich once extended an invitation to certain of his critics, but it is an invitation that, in effect, is offered to everyone—to examine his ideas with care and thoroughness and not to reject them out of hand. He likened his system to a cathedral with its many parts, its sometimes formidable exterior and its appealing interior. It is quite easy to miss the true beauty of the cathedral and not appreciate its worth if one remains only on the outside and never goes in, he said. Hence, he invited all who would, to get inside of his theological system, to look around, to get to know it before deciding for or against it.

Paul Tillich's voice has been stilled, but his ideas remain, his promise endures—and his invitation still stands.

Notes

Chapter I. Life in the Boundary Situation

1. Tillich has supplied us with several autobiographical sources which help us trace the development of his thought as well as his life: "On the Boundary: An Autobiographical Sketch," the introductory essay in *The Interpretation of History* (New York: Charles Scribner's Sons, 1936); "Author's Introduction" in *The Protestant Era* (Chicago: The University of Chicago Press, 1948); "Autobiographical Reflections" in *The Theology of Paul Tillich,* ed. Charles W. Kegley and Robert W. Bretall (New York: The Macmillan Company, 1952); "The Conquest of Intellectual Provincialism: Europe and America" in *Theology of Culture,* ed. Robert C. Kimball (New York: Oxford University Press, 1959); *On the Boundary: An Autobiographical Sketch* (New York: Charles Scribner's Sons, 1966), this work being a revision, newly translated, of the introductory essay in Tillich's *The Interpretation of History*; "Frontiers" in *The Future of Religions*, ed. Jerald C. Brauer (New York: Harper and Row, 1966); "What Am I?" in *My Search for Absolutes* (New York: Simon and Schuster, 1967), this essay being a revision of "Autobiographical Reflections" in *The Theology of Paul Tillich,* ed. Kegley and Bretall.

2. Bernard Martin, *The Existentialist Theology of Paul Tillich* (New York: Bookman Associates, 1963), p. 18.

3. Kegley and Bretall, p. 14.

4. "To Be or Not to Be," *Time*, Vol. LXIII, No. 11 (March 16, 1959), pp. 46-52.

5. Martin, p. 22.

6. Kegley and Bretall, p. 13.

7. Paul Tillich, *The Religious Situation* (New York: Henry Holt and Company, 1932), p. 85.

8. Tillich, *On the Boundary*, pp. 68-69.

9. Adolph von Harnack (1851-1930), a professor at the University of Berlin from 1889 to 1921, was an erudite church historian as well as a theologian. He is known for his seven-volume *History of Dogma* and for his *What Is Christianity?* in which he stressed the moral aspects of Christianity and the ideal of human brotherhood. Ernst Troeltsch (1865-1923), author of *The Social*

Teachings of the Christian Churches, is remembered for his religious understanding and assessment of culture. Rudolf Otto (1869-1937) wrote the classic *The Idea of the Holy*. His analysis of religion was based on an extensive knowledge of the history of religions, Oriental thought, and the natural sciences, and it focused on the numinous element in the religious consciousness.

10. Carl J. Armbruster, *The Vision of Paul Tillich* (New York: Sheed and Ward, 1967), pp. 22-23. Cf. Paul Tillich, *Systematic Theology* (Chicago: The University of Chicago Press, 1951), I, 3-8, where Tillich discusses apologetic and kerygmatic theology.

11. *The New York Times*, October 23, 1965, p. 1.

12. After using English for some years, Tillich remarked: "From the English tongue I have learned that it is not necessary to be obscure in order to be profound." One return visit to Europe is described in *My Travel Diary: 1936,* ed. Jerald C. Brauer (New York: Harper and Row, 1970). This diary provides a good deal of insight into Paul Tillich the man.

13. Kegley and Bretall, p. 17.

14. Tillich, *On the Boundary*, p. 17.

15. Kegley and Bretall, p. 7.

16. *Ibid.*, p. 19.

17. Tillich, *Theology of Culture*, pp. 164-76.

18. *Ibid.*, p. 176.

19. This incident has been reported by Tillich's friend and colleague, James Luther Adams.

20. Kegley and Bretall, p. 19.

21. Tillich, *Theology of Culture*, pp. 112-26. Here the title reads "The Theological Significance of Existentialism and Psychoanalysis."

22. *Ibid.*, p. 126.

23. Paul Tillich, "On the Boundary Line," *The Christian Century*, Vol. LXXVII, No. 49 (December 7, 1960), p. 1437.

24. "The Inner Aim," *Time*, Vol. LXXVII, No. 17 (April 21, 1961), p. 57.

25. "The Ambiguity of Perfection," *Time*, Vol. LXXXI, No. 20 (May 17, 1963), p. 69.

26. Paul Tillich, "Pacem in Terris," *Criterion*, Vol. 4, No. 2 (Spring, 1965), pp. 15-18.

27. Paul Tillich, *The Eternal Now* (New York: Charles Scribner's Sons, 1963), pp. 81-91.

28. *Ibid.*, pp. 84-86.

29. And not just Americans. Tillich's English works have been translated into German, French, Spanish, Italian, and Japanese.

30. Brauer, pp. 16-17.

31. *Ibid.*, p. 16.

32. *Ibid.*, p. 17.

33. *Ibid.*, pp. 19-20.

34. Nels F. S. Ferré *et al.*, *Paul Tillich: Retrospect and Future* (Nashville: Abingdon Press, 1966), p. 16.

35. George H. Tavard, *Paul Tillich and the Christian Message* (New York: Charles Scribner's Sons, 1962), p. 167.

36. Brauer, p. 28.

37. John Macquarrie, *Twentieth Century Religious Thought* (New York: Harper and Row, 1963), p. 374. Rudolf Bultmann is a twentieth-century existential theologian and New Testament scholar whose efforts to "demythologize" the timeless truths of the Bible attracted wide interest in the years after World War II.

38. Brauer, p. 21.

39. Rollo May was one of Tillich's students at Union Theological Seminary. The full text of his memorial address is published in *Pastoral Psychology*, Vol. 19, No. 181 (February, 1968), pp. 7-10.

Chapter II. The Theologian in the Boundary Situation: Philosophy and Theology

1. Tillich, *Systematic Theology*, I, vii. Subsequent references to this work will be abbreviated "Tillich, ST," followed by the volume and the page number.

2. *Ibid.*, I, 3.

3. *Ibid.*, p. 9.

4. Paul Tillich, *Dynamics of Faith* (New York: Harper and Row, 1957), pp. 18-21.

5. *Ibid.*, p. 1.

6. *Ibid.*; Tillich, ST, I, 11-12.

7. *Ibid.*, p. 12.

8. *Ibid.*, p. 13.

9. Tillich, ST, I, 13; Tillich, *Dynamics of Faith*, p. 2.

10. Tillich, ST, I, 14.

11. Tillich, ST, I, 35.

12. *Ibid.*, pp. 36-37.

13. *Ibid.*, pp. 38-40.

14. *Ibid.*, p. 40.

15. *Ibid.*, pp. 40-46.

16. *Ibid.*, pp. 47-52.

17. *Ibid.*, p. 50.

18. *Ibid.*, p. 18. See also Paul Tillich, *Biblical Religion and the Search for Ultimate Reality* (Chicago: The University of Chicago Press, 1955), p. 5, Tillich, *Dynamics of Faith*, p. 90.

19. Tillich, ST, I, 21.

20. *Ibid.*, p. 25.

21. Paul Tillich, *Systematic Theology* (Chicago: The University of Chicago Press, 1957), II, 30-31, quoted in Armbruster, p. 35.

22. Tillich, ST, I, 23.

23. *Ibid.*, p. 27.

24. *Ibid.*, p. 72.

25. *Ibid.*, pp. 75-79.

26. *Ibid.*, pp. 79-81.

27. For a definition of these terms and a discussion of the conflicts see Tillich, ST, I, 83-94.

28. *Ibid.*, p. 77.

29. *Ibid.*, p. 89.

30. *Ibid.*, p. 94.

31. *Ibid.*, pp. 106-18.

32. *Ibid.*, p. 110.

33. *Ibid.*

34. *Ibid.* See Martin, p. 186. Bernard Martin is quite correct in noting that Tillich has relied on Rudolf Otto's understanding of revelation as "*mysterium tremendum et fascinans.*" The *mysterium tremendum* is located in the "shock" of facing non-being; the *mysterium fascinans* is centered in the conquest of non-being by being. Of course, Tillich admits a debt to Otto. See Kegley and Bretall, p. 6.

35. Tillich, ST, I, 112.

36. *Ibid.*, pp. 116-17.

37. *Ibid.*, pp. 118-26.

38. *Ibid.*, pp. 147-55. In these pages Tillich goes to great lengths to show how revelation is able to overcome the various conflicts inherent in existential reason.

39. *Ibid.*, p. 135.

40. *Ibid.*, p. 136. See also Part V, Section II, "The Kingdom of God Within History," in Tillich's *Systematic Theology*.

41. Tillich, ST, I, 60.

Chapter III. Being and God

1. Tillich, ST, I, 163.

2. Paul Tillich, *Love, Power, and Justice* (New York: Oxford University Press, 1954), p. 19.

3. Tillich, ST, I, 164-68.

4. *Ibid.*, pp. 168-74.

5. *Ibid.*, p. 172.

6. *Ibid.*, p. 174.

7. The reader is referred to ST, I, 174-86, where Tillich presents "the ontological elements" of individualization and participation, dynamics and form, and freedom and destiny before taking up the subject of finitude.

8. *Ibid.*, pp. 188-89. What Tillich has in mind when he uses the word "non-being" is frequently hard to say. See Martin, pp. 109-10, for at least six different ways the word is used.

9. *Ibid.*, pp. 190-91.

10. *Ibid.*, p. 191.

11. These three types of anxiety are developed in Tillich's *The Courage to Be*. They are not special forms of neurotic anxiety; they do possess the "ontological quality" of anxiety as such. See Paul Tillich, *The Courage to Be* (New Haven: Yale University Press, 1952), pp. 40-54.

12. Tillich, ST, I, 191.

13. Tillich, ST, I, 204-10. Tillich cites four arguments: the ontological, moral, cosmological, and teleological.

14. *Ibid.*, p. 205.

15. *Ibid.*, p. 235.

16. *Ibid.*, p. 236.

17. *Ibid.*

18. Paul Tillich, *The Shaking of the Foundations* (New York: Charles Scribner's Sons, 1948), pp. 52-63. Cf. John A. T. Robinson, *Honest to God* (Philadelphia: The Westminster Press, 1963), pp. 45-63.

19. Tillich, *The Shaking of the Foundations*, p. 57.

20. Tillich, ST, I, 238.

21. Tillich, *Dynamics of Faith*, pp. 41-54. See also Tillich, *Theology of Culture*, pp. 53-67; Tillich, ST, I, 238-47; D. MacKenzie Brown, *Ultimate Concern: Tillich in Dialogue* (New York: Harper and Row, 1965), pp. 66-67, 87-92, 95-99, 144-49.

22. Tillich, *Theology of Culture*, pp. 59, 65.

23. Tillich, ST, I, 241-42.

24. *Ibid.*, p. 243.

25. *Ibid.*, pp. 244-45.

26. *Ibid.*

27. Tillich, *The Courage to Be*, p. 187.

28. Tillich, *Biblical Religion and the Search for Ultimate Reality*, p. 83.

29. Tillich, ST, I, 253.

30. Tillich prefers the term "supranaturalism" to "supernaturalism," though he does not offer an explanation for this usage. It has been proposed that "supra" connotes the "above" position, while "super" has overtones of power. Therefore, "supranatural" would be more suitable for Tillich's purpose. Tillich thus objects to supranatu-

ralism because it places God above the world. See Armbruster, p. 163.

31. Some examples of his opposition are found in: ST, I, 64-65, 116-17; ST, II, 5-6; ST, III, 5; *The Protestant Era*, p. 151; Kegley and Bretall, p. 341.

32. Tillich, *The Protestant Era*, p. 82.

33. Tillich, ST, II, 7.

Chapter IV. Existence and the Christ

1. Paul Tillich, *The New Being* (New York: Charles Scribner's Sons, 1955), p. 15.

2. Tillich, ST, II, 20-21.

3. *Ibid.*, p. 25.

4. *Ibid.*, pp. 29-44.

5. *Ibid.*, p. 31.

6. *Ibid.*, p. 38.

7. *Ibid.*, pp. 44-47.

8. *Ibid.*, pp. 44-45.

9. *Ibid.*, p. 45.

10. *Ibid.*, pp. 47-55.

11. *Ibid.*, p. 56.

12. *Ibid.*, pp. 79-80.

13. *Ibid.*, pp. 80-86.

14. *Ibid.*, pp. 86-90.

15. *Ibid.*, pp. 97-99. Some of the phrases Tillich employs are "Jesus who is called the Christ," "Jesus as the Christ," or merely, "Jesus the Christ."

16. *Ibid.*, pp. 99-118.

17. A phrase made famous by the title of Albert Schweitzer's celebrated work, *The Quest for the Historical Jesus*.

18. Tillich, ST, II, 114.

19. *Ibid.*, p. 115.

20. *Ibid.*, pp. 121-25.

21. *Ibid.*, p. 119.

22. *Ibid.*, p. 131.

23. *Ibid.*, pp. 128-29.

24. *Ibid.*, p. 126.

25. His death anxiety is not removed; it is taken into participation in the "will of God." His homelessness and insecurity are accepted in the power of a participation in a "transcendent place." Error and doubt are taken into participation in the divine life and thus indirectly into the divine omniscience, etc. *Ibid.*, p. 134. Also, see Martin, pp. 165-66.

26. Tillich, ST, II, 141. Cf. Paul Tillich, *A History of Christian Thought* (New York: Harper and Row, 1968), pp. 79-90.

27. Tillich, ST, II, 148.

28. *Ibid.*, p. 149. Tillich also feels the phrase, "Logos [the Word] became flesh," is misleading, unless it is read in a very specific way. See ST, II, 95.

29. *Ibid.*, p. 148. See Guyton B. Hammond, *The Power of Self-Transcendence* (St. Louis: The Bethany Press, 1966), p. 84, for a helpful and clear exposition of this concept.

30. Tillich reaches back to the polarity of freedom-destiny to say that both Jesus' admission of his destiny as the Messiah and his complete freedom to follow or refuse his destiny are factors in a proper Christology. Such freedom, with risks and dangers included, points to an adoptionist Christology, Tillich admits. That does not concern him unduly, for both incarnational and adoptionist Christologies have Biblical roots, and an incarnational Christology needs an adoptionist one—and vice versa. See Tillich, ST, II, 148-49.

31. *Ibid.*, pp. 150-53.

32. *Ibid.*, pp. 153-55.

33. *Ibid.*, pp. 155-58.

34. *Ibid.*, p. 157.

35. *Ibid.*

36. Tillich, *The Shaking of the Foundations*, p. 172.

37. Tillich, ST, II, 166.

38. *Ibid.*, pp. 167-68.

39. *Ibid.*, pp. 173-76.

40. *Ibid.*, pp. 176-80.

41. Tillich, *The Shaking of the Foundations*, p. 162.

Chapter V. Life and the Spirit

1. Paul Tillich, *Systematic Theology* (Chicago: The University of Chicago Press, 1963), III, 12.

2. *Ibid.*, pp. 12-17.

3. *Ibid.*, p. 22. Tillich's practice is consistent throughout: spirit (small "s") refers to man's spirit; Spirit (capital "s") to God's spirit.

4. *Ibid.*, p. 27.

5. Tillich, *The Shaking of the Foundations*, p. 137.

6. Tillich, ST, III, 30-106.

7. *Ibid.*, pp. 30-32. See also Alexander McKelway, *The Systematic Theology of Paul Tillich* (Richmond, Virginia: John Knox Press, 1964), pp. 192-98, for one of the clearest interpretations of Tillich's "Self-Actualization of Life and Its Ambiguities."

8. Tillich, ST, III, 32.

9. *Ibid.*, pp. 107-10.

10. *Ibid.*, p. 107.

11. *Ibid.*, pp. 111-12.

12. *Ibid.*, pp. 129, 138.

13. *Ibid.*, pp. 149-50.

14. *Ibid.*, pp. 150-57.

15. *Ibid.*, p. 152.

16. *Ibid.*, p. 154. Cf. Tillich, *The Protestant Era*, p. xvii. The distinction between latent and manifest community also includes a "before" and "after" character—"before" the encounter with the New Being in Jesus as the Christ (latent), "after" this encounter (manifest).

17. Tillich, ST, III, 158. See also Tillich, *The Protestant Era*, p. xiii.

18. Tillich, ST, III, 159.

19. *Ibid.*, pp. 162-65.

20. Tillich criticizes the pre-Vatican II Catholic Church for trying to ignore the ambiguities of life and submerge the sociological character in its theological character. *Ibid.*, pp. 166-67.

21. *Ibid.*, p. 165.

22. *Ibid.*, p. 167.

23. *Ibid.*, p. 172.

24. *Ibid.*, pp. 182-87.

25. Tillich adds another kind of function—the "relating function" of the churches, which governs the churches' encounters with other sociological groups. *Ibid.*, pp. 212-16.

26. *Ibid.*, p. 217.

27. *Ibid.*, pp. 221-28.

28. *Ibid.*, pp. 231-37.

29. *Ibid.*, pp. 243-44.

30. Tillich, *The Protestant Era*, p. 163.

31. Tillich, ST, III, 245. See also Tillich, *The Protestant Era*, pp. 222-33. Here he puts the question, "The End of the Protestant Era?" as the title of a chapter. He does not supply a final answer to the question, though he looks for Protestantism to have a rough time of it in the modern world as it faces the threats of Communism, nationalism, and Catholicism. The most important consideration, however, is not whether the Protestant era is over or not. It is that the *Protestant principle* will never die.

32. Tillich, ST, III, 245-65. See also Tillich, *The Protestant Era*, pp. 44-48, 56-65.

33. Tillich, ST, III, 258-59.

34. *Ibid.*

35. Tillich, *The Protestant Era*, p. 57.

36. Hammond, p. 95.

37. Tillich, ST, III, 252.

38. It is only after the discussion on the Spiritual Presence that Tillich feels it is proper to take up the doctrine of the Trinity. See the section, "The Trinitarian Symbols," ST, III, 283-94.

Chapter VI. History and the Kingdom of God

1. Tillich, *Theology of Culture*, p. 37.

2. Tillich, ST, III, 297-99. Many of Tillich's ideas on history in this part of his system were developed earlier in Parts Two, Three, and Four of *The Interpretation of History*.

3. Tillich, ST, III, 300.

4. *Ibid.*, p. 304.

5. *Ibid.*, pp. 302-6.

6. *Ibid.*, p. 308.

7. *Ibid.*, pp. 308-11.

8. *Ibid.*, p. 312.

9. Tillich, *The Shaking of the Foundations*, p. 37.

10. Tillich, ST, III, 320.

11. *Ibid.*

12. *Ibid.*, p. 336.

13. *Ibid.*, p. 340.

14. *Ibid.*, p. 343.

15. *Ibid.*, p. 344.

16. *Ibid.*, p. 349.

17. *Ibid.*, pp. 349-50. Tillich does not arrive at his answer of the "Kingdom of God" quite so abruptly. He contrasts this symbol with two general types of competing interpretations, the negative, nonhistorical and the positive, historical. See Tillich, ST, III, 350-56.

18. *Ibid.*, p. 357.

19. *Ibid.*, pp. 358-59.

20. *Ibid.*, p. 364.

21. *Ibid.*

22. *Ibid.*, pp. 365-66.

23. *Ibid.*, p. 364.

24. *Ibid.*, pp. 369-72. See also Tillich, *The Protestant Era*, pp. 27-28, 32-51, 155-56. Tillich contrasts *kairos* with *chronos*, wherein the latter term signifies measured time and the former stresses a quality of time, not the quantitative side.

25. Tillich, ST, III, 370, 372.

26. *Ibid.*, p. 371.

27. *Ibid.*

28. *Ibid.*, p. 377.

29. *Ibid.*
30. *Ibid.*, pp. 385-93.
31. *Ibid.*, p. 394.
32. Tillich, *The Shaking of the Foundations*, p. 23.
33. Tillich, ST, III, 402.
34. *Ibid.*, pp. 406-8.
35. Tillich will allow the term "immortality" if by this "the power of essentialization" is understood. In no case will he permit "immortality" if it is conceived as the continuation of the temporal life of a person after death minus a body. *Ibid.*, pp. 409-10. See also Tillich, *The Eternal Now*, pp. 114-15, 124-25.
36. Tillich, ST, III, 412-13.
37. *Ibid.*, p. 413.
38. *Ibid.*, p. 421.
39. *Ibid.*, p. 420.
40. Tillich, *The Eternal Now*, p. 114.

Chapter VII. Looking Back and Looking Forward

1. Brauer, pp. 52-63.
2. *Ibid.*, pp. 53-57.
3. See the Bibliography for some of the major critical statements on Tillich's work.
4. Kenneth Hamilton, *The System and the Gospel* (New York: The Macmillan Company, 1963), p. 227.
5. Tillich, ST, III, 3-7.
6. Hammond, p. 109.
7. Tillich, ST, III, 4.
8. From "An Introductory Report by Karl Barth," McKelway, p. 13. For more on Tillich and Barth, see David Hopper, *Tillich: A Theological Portrait* (Philadelphia: J. B. Lippincott Company, 1968).
9. Armbruster, p. 293.
10. Edward A. Dowey, Jr., "Tillich, Barth, and the Criteria of Theology," *Theology Today*, XV (April, 1958), p. 57, quoted in Armbruster, p. 294.
11. Cf. J. Heywood Thomas, *Paul Tillich: An Appraisal* (Philadelphia: The Westminster Press, 1963); Hamilton, *The System and the Gospel*; George H. Tavard, *Paul Tillich and the Christian Message* (New York: Charles Scribner's Sons, 1962).
12. It is reported that he once told a group of Japanese Buddhists it was a matter of indifference to him as a Christian theologian whether or not Jesus lived. See Ferré *et al.*, p. 7.
13. Hamilton, p. 164.
14. Tillich, ST, II, 98.

15. *Ibid.*, p. 94. See also Brown, pp. 153-56, 211-13, where Tillich discusses the image and reality of Jesus, and where he confesses to his indecision as to whether picture or image is the better term.

16. Nels F. S. Ferré, "The Fabric of Paul Tillich's Theology," *Scottish Journal of Theology*, Vol. 21, No. 2 (June, 1968), pp. 164-65.

17. On Tillich's use of symbol, see Hammond, pp. 110-21; David H. Kelsey, *The Fabric of Paul Tillich's Theology* (New Haven: Yale University Press, 1967); George H. Tavard, *Paul Tillich and the Christian Message* (New York: Charles Scribner's Sons, 1962), pp. 82-112; William L. Rowe, *Religious Symbols and God* (Chicago: The University of Chicago Press, 1968). On faith and doubt, see especially Robert P. Scharlemann, *Reflection and Doubt in the Thought of Paul Tillich* (New Haven: Yale University Press, 1969).

18. John Dillenberger, "Paul Tillich: Theologian of Culture," in Ferré *et al.*, p. 39.

19. Ved Mehta, *The New Theologian* (New York: Harper and Row, 1965), p. 68.

20. My debt to Langdon Gilkey for this particular expression of Tillich's promise is as deep as it is obvious. See Langdon Gilkey, *Naming the Whirlwind: The Renewal of God-Language* (Indianapolis: The Bobbs-Merrill Company, 1970), pp. 454-57. Gilkey himself has written, "One of the most creative, and universally illustrated, contributions of Paul Tillich to theological discussion has been his 'method of correlation' between the questions which ordinary existence raises and the answers which the Christian message provides." *Ibid.*, p. 455.

21. Robert N. Bellah, *Beyond Belief* (New York: Harper and Row, 1970), p. 245.

22. *Ibid.*, p. 255.

23. Walter Leibrecht, "The Life and Mind of Paul Tillich," in *Religion and Culture: Essays in Honor of Paul Tillich*, ed. Walter Leibrecht (New York: Harper and Brothers, 1959), p. 17.

24. Paul Tillich, "On the Boundary Line," *The Christian Century*, Vol. LXXVII, No. 49 (December 7, 1960), p. 1435.

25. *Ibid.*

26. Paul Tillich, *Christianity and the Encounter of the World Religions* (New York: Columbia University Press, 1963), p. 64.

27. *Ibid.*, p. 96.

28. *Ibid.*, p. 97.

29. Brauer, pp. 80-94.

30. *Ibid.*, p. 86.

31. *Ibid.*, p. 91.

A Selected Bibliography

Books by Paul Tillich

Biblical Religion and the Search for Ultimate Reality. Chicago: The University of Chicago Press, 1955.

    Tillich relates the Bible to philosophy and attempts to show that each of the Biblical symbols pushes on to an ontological question.

Christianity and the Encounter of the World Religions. New York: Columbia University Press, 1963.

    An examination of the relationship between Christianity and non-Christian religions, including quasi-religions such as nationalism and socialism. The relationship between Christianity and Buddhism is singled out for special treatment.

The Courage to Be. New Haven: Yale University Press, 1952.

    The experience of anxiety is described in some detail. Then the various meanings of courage in the history of Western thought are presented, followed by Tillich's discussion of the power of being as the source of "the courage to be."

The Dynamics of Faith. New York: Harper and Brothers, 1957.

    A perceptive analysis of what faith is and is not, including a discussion of religious symbols. The practical consequences of faith are not overlooked. This is one place to begin a study of Tillich's thought.

The Eternal Now. New York: Charles Scribner's Sons, 1963.

    Sermons of Tillich under the three main headings of "The Human Predicament," "The Divine Reality," and "The Challenge to Man."

The Future of Religions. Edited by Jerald C. Brauer. New York: Harper and Row, 1966.

    Contains four important, later essays by Tillich, the fourth being his final public lecture, along with three tributes to Tillich by Brauer, Wilhelm Pauck, and Mircea Eliade, read at the Tillich Memorial Service at the University of Chicago in October, 1965, and sixteen pages of photographs of Tillich by Archie Lieberman.

A History of Christian Thought. Edited by Carl E. Braaten. New York: Harper and Row, 1968.

Tillich's course lectures, surveying the history of Christian thought from the time of Christ to the time of Protestant Orthodoxy, Pietism, and the Enlightenment, originally delivered at Union Theological Seminary in 1953.

The Interpretation of History. New York: Charles Scribner's Sons, 1936.

An earlier work which includes some biographical information as well as a discussion of some of Tillich's ideas on history, such as *kairos*, theonomy, and the demonic.

Love, Power, and Justice. New York: Oxford University Press, 1954.

A rather abstract treatment of the "ontological analyses and ethical applications" of these three main moral qualities; in short, Tillich's social philosophy.

Morality and Beyond. New York: Harper and Row, 1963.

A collection of essays comprising a brief, but good introduction to Tillich's ethics. The thesis is that man's moral concerns finally have meaning only when they are put in the context of his relationship to God.

My Search for Absolutes. New York: Simon and Schuster, 1967.

A revision of an earlier essay, "Autobiographical Reflections," originally published in *The Theology of Paul Tillich,* edited by Kegley and Bretall (see below). Illustrated with drawings by Saul Steinberg.

My Travel Diary: 1936. Edited by Jerald C. Brauer. New York: Harper and Row, 1970.

After living in the United States for nearly three years, Tillich returned to Europe and Great Britain for a brief visit. The diary, designed initially to inform Tillich's wife of the people he met and the events he experienced, provides a good deal of insight into Tillich the man. Illustrated with drawings by Alfonso Ossorio.

The New Being. New York: Charles Scribner's Sons, 1955.

Sermons preached mainly in colleges and universities, together furnishing a kind of answer to the questions raised in *The Shaking of the Foundations.* The stress is on the New Being, the new state of things, made possible with the appearance of Jesus as the Christ.

On the Boundary: An Autobiographical Sketch. New York: Charles Scribner's Sons, 1966.

A revision of the introductory essay in *The Interpretation of History,* showing how the boundary stance was so vital for Tillich.

Perspectives on 19th and 20th Century Protestant Theology. Edited by Carl E. Braaten. New York: Harper and Row, 1967.

Lectures delivered at the Divinity School of the University

of Chicago in 1963. Topics and theologians treated extend from Protestant Orthodoxy and Pietism to Bultmann and Barth, including such non-Protestant theologians as Marx and Nietzsche. This volume complements *A History of Christian Thought*, since both together present Tillich's sweep of the classical Christian tradition.

The Protestant Era. Chicago: The University of Chicago Press, 1948 (Abridged edition, A Phoenix Book, paperback, 1957).

A collection of essays from Tillich's earlier period, many of them published before he came to America, treating a number of themes relating to culture, history, ethics, and the like. There are two valuable introductions, one by Tillich and one by James Luther Adams, the translator.

ıe Religious Situation. New York: Henry Holt and Company, 1932.

This, too, comes from Tillich's German period, being chiefly a discussion of issues in European life in the years following World War I. Tillich analyzes the religious situation in science, art, politics, ethics, and in the churches themselves.

The Shaking of the Foundations. New York: Charles Scribner's Sons, 1948.

This is yet another volume of Tillich's sermons. He attempts to be Biblical and yet not to employ Biblical and ecclesiastical terminology as he addresses himself to personal and social problems. This group of sermons, along with *The Eternal Now* and *The New Being*, would be another advantageous introduction to Tillich for the beginner.

Systematic Theology. Chicago: The University of Chicago Press.

This work represents Tillich's definitive theological position, although it is not easy reading for the novice. Available in one volume, it is also obtainable in three separate volumes. Volume I (1951) includes Tillich's introduction to his system and the parts, "Reason and Revelation" and "Being and God." Volume II (1957) includes Tillich's analysis of human existence and the doctrine of Christ. Volume III (1963) deals with the ambiguities of life and history and their resolution in the life of the Spirit and in the Kingdom of God, and discusses the doctrines of the church and eschatology.

Theology of Culture. Edited by Robert C. Kimball. New York: Oxford University Press, 1959.

Important essays from the 1940s and 1950s which, in one way or another, uphold Tillich's conviction that genuine religion is never divorced from the main stream of culture.

Ultimate Concern: Tillich in Dialogue. Edited by D. Mackenzie Brown. New York: Harper and Row, 1965.

Tape recordings of Tillich's conversations with students, professors, and clergy on a variety of themes at the University of California, Santa Barbara, in 1964. This, too, constitutes a good place to begin a study of the man and his theology.

What Is Religion? Edited by James L. Adams. New York: Harper and Row, 1969.

A reprinting of three major essays on Tillich's philosophy of religion which were originally published in Germany in the years 1919-25. The editor has supplied a helpful introduction.

A full bibliography of Tillich's writings covering the years 1910-58 has been compiled by Peter H. John and is published in *Religion and Culture: Essays in Honor of Paul Tillich*, edited by Walter Leibrecht (New York: Harper and Brothers, 1959), pp. 367-96.

Books About Paul Tillich

Adams, James Luther. *Paul Tillich's Philosophy of Culture, Science, and Religion.* New York: Harper and Row, 1965.

An excellent scholarly study of these aspects of Tillich's thought in his German period. Moderately difficult for the general reader.

Armbruster, Carl J. *The Vision of Paul Tillich.* New York: Sheed and Ward, 1967.

A very careful and thorough examination by a Catholic scholar of Tillich's theology, based on the conviction that Tillich's analysis of the relation of religion to culture is his most significant contribution.

Hamilton, Kenneth. *The System and the Gospel.* New York: The Macmillan Company, 1963.

A critique of Tillich's system that is more negative than positive, but at the same time provocative in its thrust.

Hammond, Guyton B. *The Power of Self-Transcendence.* St. Louis: The Bethany Press, 1966.

A shorter introduction to some of the major themes in Tillich's thought by one who is largely sympathetic with Tillich's intent.

Hopper, David. *Tillich: A Theological Portrait.* Philadelphia: J. B. Lippincott Company, 1968.

A study of Tillich which does not pretend to be comprehensive but instead concentrates on the differences between Barth and Tillich.

Kegley, Charles W., and Robert W. Bretall (eds.). *The Theology of Paul Tillich.* New York: The Macmillan Company, 1952.

A fine collection of critical articles based on Tillich's works up to 1952, including an autobiographical essay by Tillich.

Kelsey, David H. *The Fabric of Paul Tillich's Theology.* New Haven: Yale University Press, 1967.

A work which focuses on Tillich's theological statements, particularly in his sermons, rather than on an explication of his system.

Leibrecht, Walter (ed.). *Religion and Culture: Essays in Honor of Paul Tillich.* New York: Harper and Brothers, 1959.

The editor has written a perceptive essay on Tillich's life and thought, and the book concludes with Peter John's bibliography of Tillich's writings through 1958, though the essays themselves are not directed to Tillich's thought as such.

McKelway, Alexander J. *The Systematic Theology of Paul Tillich.* Richmond: John Knox Press, 1964.

A fair and accurate exposition of Tillich's *Systematic Theology* from one who finally is more sympathetic to Barth than to Tillich.

Martin, Bernard. *The Existentialist Theology of Paul Tillich.* New York: Bookman Associates, 1963.

A faithful introduction to the concepts found in the first two volumes of *Systematic Theology* by a Jewish scholar.

O'Meara, Thomas A., and Celestin D. Weisser (eds.). *Paul Tillich in Catholic Thought.* Dubuque: The Priory Press, 1964.

Catholic appraisals of Tillich which add to the reader's understanding of Tillich and of current trends in Catholic theology. Tillich has included an afterword.

Rowe, William L. *Religious Symbols and God.* Chicago: The University of Chicago Press, 1968.

A mildly critical treatment of Tillich's use of religious symbols and ontological statements by one who views Tillich more as a philosopher seeking to explain the religious dimension of human existence than as a theologian writing a theology for the church.

Scharlemann, Robert P. *Reflection and Doubt in the Thought of Paul Tillich.* New Haven: Yale University Press, 1969.

A scholarly discussion of many of Tillich's main ideas, with special attention given to reflection and doubt, followed by Scharlemann's evaluation and appreciation in the concluding chapter.

Tavard, George H. *Paul Tillich and the Christian Message.* New York: Charles Scribner's Sons, 1962.

A study of Tillich's Christology by a Catholic scholar who knows his way around in Tillich but who finds his Christology lacking on certain counts.

Thomas, J. Heywood. *Paul Tillich: An Appraisal.* Philadelphia: The Westminster Press, 1963.

The author comes at Tillich by way of linguistic philosophy and is critical of him at a number of points.